Advice to the Minister of Music

Get a Giant Hat Rack!

Chéri Walters

CHRISM

02-0339

In memory of Rev. Floyd W. Lee, "the leader of the band."
Grandpa, "your blood runs through my instrument and your
song is in my soul." Thanks for the genes!

©1994 by Gospel Publishing House, Springfield, Missouri 65802-1894.
All rights reserved. No part of this book may be reproduced, stored in a
retrieval system, or transmitted in any form or by any means—electronic, mechanical, photocopy, recording, or otherwise—without prior
written permission of the copyright owner, except brief quotations used
in connection with reviews in magazines or newspapers.

Chrism Books are published by Gospel Publishing House.

Library of Congress Cataloging-in-Publication Data

Walters, Chéri.
    Advice to the minister of music: get a giant hat rack! / Chéri Walters.
        p.   cm.
    "02-0339."
    Includes bibliographical references.
    ISBN 0-88243-339-3
    1. Ministers of music.   2. Church music.   I. Title.
    ML3001.W35   1994   93-48853
    264' .2—dc20

Printed in the United States of America

Contents

Preface

You may wonder how I came to wear the music minister's hat. It's all my mom's fault.

You see, she gave me the music minister genes. As long as I can remember, she's been playing the church piano and we've been singing in church. Mom and all four of her brothers have been choir directors at one time or another, plus directed their own gospel quartets or groups. Their father, my grandfather, was a preacher who was at least half musician; he sang tenor, could play just about every instrument, and taught "singing schools" back in the days of shaped notes and all-day singin' on the grounds. His father (and maybe his father before him) also traveled around teaching less fortunate souls—those who didn't already have music in their genes—how to read shaped notes and sing harmony.

And it's in my kids' genes, too. I'll never forget when my husband, Ken, took our then-four-year-old son to see *Star Wars*. About halfway through the movie, Paul leaned over, eyes wide, and whispered, "Daddy! Darth Vader's coming!"

Ken knew Paul hadn't seen the picture before. "How do you know, Paul?" he asked surprised.

With the elaborate patience that only a four-year-old can muster, Paul explained to his father: "Because, Daddy, they're playing his music."

Ken, who is no slouch musically himself, began to listen to the

4

film score. Sure enough, each major character had a theme, and they were indeed playing "Darth Vader's music."

I'm telling you, it's in the genes.

So what does that have to do with this book? Well, besides giving me a chance to brag about my family, it will show you why I thought that if anybody was ever prepared to be a minister of music it was me.

I knew when I went to college that I would be a music major. I never wanted to be anything else. I never went through those long sophomore soul searches trying to decide what major to declare. I also knew that my boyfriend (who became my husband by my junior year) was planning to be a pastor. So I took the church music road.

Less than a month out of college, Ken and I joined our first church staff. He was the assistant pastor and I was the part-time secretary and the music minister. With a church music diploma in my hand, church music heritage in my heart, and church music genes coursing through my veins, I was ready!

The problem is, church music ministry is so much more than selecting, rehearsing, singing, and conducting music. If I'd had to wear only the church musician's hat, I really would have been almost as ready as I thought I was.

But they didn't tell me in Church Music Administration 101 how to deal with Barry, who dropped out of choir when I unwittingly offended him, or Donna, who thought I was discriminating against her daughter when she didn't make it through the Christmas Tree auditions. My Hymnology and Liturgy class gave me a broad perspective on designing an order of worship but was no help at all when it came to recruiting and motivating people to stay through a late choir rehearsal when they had to get up at four-thirty in the morning for work.

I learned some wonderful things in college, many of which continue to influence my ministry today. But I was completely unprepared for how many different hats I would have to wear, like the manager's hat with its budgeting, accounting, and cataloging responsibilities, or the sound technician's hat with its mysteries of ohms and impedance. Since graduation I've learned a lot about those other hats from colleagues in music ministry, from workshops and seminars, from books and articles, but mostly I learned them from cold, hard experience.

And that's what this book is about: sharing some of my experiences, and those of my learned colleagues and painfully honest friends, in hopes that it might spare you some coldness and hardness in your experiences.

Throughout this book we'll take a close look at several of the hats that music ministers wear. Some of those hats, like the musician's hat or the staff member's hat, one might expect. Other hats, like the counselor's hat or manager's hat, can come as a rude shock.

One of our primary objectives in ministry should be to find and train others to take on some of the responsibilities in the music ministry. So choose the two or three hats on your hat rack that only you can wear, that only you are called to wear. Then begin to pray and prepare, plant seeds and bend twigs (we'll talk about how later), and hand the remaining hats to others who can wear them.

The first and most important hat we'll look at is the minister's hat. For me, music ministry is not a career choice but a calling. It has also proven to be quite a juggling act, and we'll discuss the difficulties of trying to balance ministry responsibilities with family and personal needs.

The second hat we'll take down is the staff member's hat. We will turn it around and look at our relationship with the senior pastor and with other staff members and examine the trust that holds a staff together.

Next is one of those hats for which I was least prepared, the counselor's hat. I had no idea how much ministry simply meant dealing with people—hurting, vulnerable, imperfect, frustrating people, who still often manage to model Christ in the most surprising, unexpected ways.

The communicator's hat is one I think will become increasingly important in our information age. As Christians, we're all communicators of the gospel; as Christian musicians, we've chosen music as our vehicle to get the gospel across. As music ministers, we need to learn to communicate effectively not only music techniques but also our goals and visions.

To implement those goals and visions we have to put on the manager's hat and organize, schedule, and plan the elements that make up our music ministries.

Another hat I wear more than I'd ever dreamed is the talent

agent's hat. It seems I spend half my time recruiting and training choir and worship team members, light technicians, children's choir workers, drama team members, costume seamstresses, assistant directors, and more. But this is a critical role if you ever intend to give away some of your hats.

Then there's the producer's hat. I see this one becoming even more important as the church tries to reach an increasingly visually-oriented society. I remember when I was a kid in church the choir wore robes, stood up in the loft, and sang the Christmas cantata while holding their books. Now there are so many more elements available to get the message across—choreography, video, drama, costuming and staging, sign language, banners—it's not just a musical anymore, it's a production!

Another hat you may not have expected to wear is the sound technician's hat. Even if you have qualified personnel to run your sound, it doesn't hurt to get acquainted with the basics and learn some of the vocabulary.

And the last hat? Why, the musician's hat, of course. It's the one I started out most prepared for, but maybe you're like some of my friends in music ministry who came from a drama background or who majored in Christian education and got music thrown into their portfolio. Or maybe you're one of those responsible, dedicated, heroic people who were asked to fill in as temporary choir director and found out it was a permanent position. My hat is off to you!

I've told many friends that this book took longer to bring into the world than a baby—and the labor was harder! To all my friends and family who believed me when I wrote in all those Christmas letters about this book, thank you!

I'm humbled when I think of the many people in the California, Florida, and Oklahoma churches who have touched my life and made it richer. I've seen Jesus in your faces and heard Him in your voices. Thank you.

I'd like to acknowledge the national Music Department staff, past and present, as well as Silas Gaither and Terry Raburn for their solid support of this project. I'm especially grateful to Dan ("E. S.") Crace who came into the project in the middle and became head cheerleader, and to Carmen Wassam who has been "in the kitchen" with me since the beginning. You all kept me going, guys!

Most of all, thanks to my big wonderful musical family (you all know who you are): Mike; Anne; Dale; Sher; my parents, Glen and Jane Davis (and two of my biggest fans); my kids, Paul, Andrea, Brienne, and Skylar; and to my husband, Ken (the other biggest fan), who also is my partner in ministry. Together with Jesus we make a great team, Babe!

Introduction

Even though music holds first place in our hearts, many music ministers do double and triple duty overseeing the youth and music programs or the music and Christian education programs or the music, youth, and Christian education programs.

One friend laughingly describes his first staff position as minister of music and maintenance. It seems the church needed a custodian and since they couldn't afford to pay him a full-time salary as music minister . . . well, you guessed it.

After I served as part-time church secretary and part-time music minister at my first church, I swore I'd never do it again. Ten years later my husband became the pastor of a small church and guess what? There I was, typing the bulletin again when I wanted to be listening to new choral releases!

Alas, some hats you choose to wear and some are forced upon you. But there are a few hats you will want to avoid.

Hats to Keep Off Your Head

The Policeman's Hat

The policeman, also known as the dictator, has the sense of humor and diplomacy you usually associate with a Marine Corps boot camp sergeant. He throws tantrums, batons, music, music stands—and only his superhuman discipline has kept him from throwing that gossipy, gum-popping soprano in the first row.

The policeman also deploys nonphysical weapons like humiliation techniques and good old-fashioned yelling and screaming. His arsenal of put-downs and snappy comebacks is unmatched. Not that he enjoys it, mind you. As one Old World European conductor, noted for hurling insults and batons at his philharmonic orchestra, explained, "They *make* me do it!"

The Martyr's Hat

Unlike the policeman, the martyr does not inflict pain on the choir members but upon himself. He bangs his head against the podium, the piano, the timpani, the wall—whatever is most dramatic at the moment. Dress rehearsals can nearly land him in the intensive care unit.

You see, somewhere along the line, the martyr came to the conclusion that guilt motivates people. Probably when his mother said, "And after all I've done for you, this is the thanks I get." He interprets "weeping and wailing and gnashing of teeth" to be a biblical command, particularly to those in positions of leadership.

The Mother's Hat

I want to make it clear that you do not have to be either a woman or a parent to be a mother. It just takes what is called in transactional analysis parent-to-child communication. The music minister plays the role of the parent, treating the choir members as children.

The mother alternates between scolding ("Now stop talking and pay attention, choir") and cajoling ("Let's make our pastor and congregation proud of us"), with a little of the martyr's guilt thrown in for good measure ("You know it makes me unhappy when you don't watch me").

This parent-to-child style of communication is also frequently used by doctors with their patients ("And how are we doing today?") and by postal employees with almost everyone ("This window is closed. Can't you read?").

Like your own mother, this type of music minister is by turns either warm and comforting or totally frustrating.

The Superstar's Hat

The superstar has arrived at the highest echelon of choir directordom. He's the guy or gal we all read about (with our green-tinted glasses on) in those church music magazines. He's more like a Hollywood mogul than the director of a church choir. He's got assistants; secretaries; assistant secretaries; secretarial assistants; lighting, sound, and special effects crews—even key grips (whatever they are)!

The superstar is also a legend in his own mind. He's the featured soloist in every musical and the star in every production. If he could play all twelve disciples, plus Jesus, he'd do his own living Last Supper.

Of course, he didn't soar right out of Bible college and land in a megachurch. He probably had to work his way up. Who knows—maybe he was even a key grip.

The Halo

The halo can be worn only by someone who is so spiritual, so holy, he's above the rest of the music department, yea, verily, even above the rest of the pastoral staff.

He's got all the answers to all those troubling theological questions like, "How many angels can fit on the head of a pin?" and "Did Adam have a belly button?" He's the bionic believer, able to leap from one out-of-context Scripture verse to another in a single bound.

He knows the secret sin of everyone in his choir and goes about exhorting and admonishing them until they are sick unto death of him. Trouble is, he's so busy plucking the splinters out of others' eyes that he can't see the beam in his own.

The Superhuman's Hat

This hat is the heaviest, the most crushing of all. It's all the other hats combined and then some. The superhuman thinks he has to be all and do all, and his self-sufficiency is going to land him in either the cardiac unit, divorce court, or a padded cell.

Superhuman needs to realize that although God calls each of us individually, He doesn't call us to minister alone. Part of our job description as ministers is "to equip the saints" (Ephesians

4:12, NRSV; read, "giving away some of your hats"), and you'd think musicians above all would understand that. After all, what is harmony but a number of individuals each carrying his own part yet blending with the others so that the sum is greater than its parts. Harmony is something the greatest soloist can't produce.

Check Your Mirror

We've looked at some hat wearers who are exaggerations and, I hope, had a good laugh at their expense. But we looked at them first because we can learn from them. Unfortunately, there are times when all of us are tempted to wear some of their hats. It's hard to resist being a little holier-than-thou sometimes. It's hard not to slip into the mother's hat and say "I told you so" to that chronically late soprano whose tardiness made her miss out on the solo auditions. It's tempting to give yourself that climactic solo in the Christmas musical when you know you can do it better than anyone else. It's difficult to keep your tongue in check when time is running out and the choir still hasn't buckled down to learn the music.

Granted, all of us are human beings. If we've been in ministry for more than a few minutes, all of us have said or done things we wish we could unsay or undo. But we need to take a good, hard look at ourselves and make sure that temper tantrums or guilt prods aren't part of our regular method of operation.

Perhaps because I'm a woman I try to be particularly careful not to come off as somebody's mother. I especially don't want the men I work with to view me as another Mrs. Jones, my high school composition teacher who sat at her desk scowling at the class with half-glasses perched on the end of her nose.

I suppose the bottom line is that we must treat those within our circle of ministry with respect, recognizing that all of us, from the senior pastor to the most recent convert, are pilgrims on the same journey. Like John Bunyan's Christian in *Pilgrim's Progress,* we're making our way toward Celestial City, perhaps some with detours or delays. Our purpose is not to scold or condemn but to encourage, to set an example, even to carry each other if necessary. The pilgrim in each of us needs to remind the musician in each of us that music is not our reason for being.

What matters is the people we bring with us and the Lord at journey's end.

"Some of the loftiest aspirations of the human soul are reserved to those who have the great gift of musical expression, for they thereby lift themselves out of a material world and enter a spiritual one."

—Fritz Kreisler

Think of those few, brief, shining moments in worship services or concerts when everything gels. The music comes together, the voices blend, the Spirit breathes, and we know we've touched God. For just a little while, the fog that restricts our vision to the ordinary and the mundane lifts, and we get a glimpse of something eternal and immortal. Savor those moments and store them up for days when the accompanist doesn't show up for service and doesn't call, or the whole bass section decides the play-offs are more important than the dress rehearsal. Those shining moments, those glimpses of eternity, remind us during times of discouragement or frustration that "this too shall pass." It won't always be like this, not here, and especially not in heaven.

"The occupation of heaven is praise."

—John Masefield

Plenty of Scripture verses tell us there will be music and singing in heaven. Praise will be our chief occupation. I'm looking forward to that! There will be heavenly music, heavenly musicians, the choir to end all choirs, and everybody will be at all the rehearsals! Come to think of it, we probably won't need rehearsals—it'll just be one long opening night. I don't know who will get to conduct that group, but wouldn't it be fun if we all got a turn?

Till then, my advice is to get a giant hat rack. We'll look at ways to wear our hats well and to train others to wear some of them. But let's keep one eye on the final goal—that's when we get to turn in all our hats for a crown!

♪

1

The Minister's Hat

The Call to Ministry

Why do you want to be a minister?" The two presbyters and one theology professor who formed my ministerial credentials interview committee waited for my answer.

"I can't do anything else," I told them.

Now, I know there are two ways to take that statement: "I can't *do* anything else" as in, "I don't know how"; but I meant, "I can*not* do anything else" as in, "I feel incomplete outside of ministry."

My husband and I have both on occasion had to supplement our ministry incomes by working secular jobs. Each time, we've met wonderful people, gained valuable experience, and learned a lot. But we were like fish out of water; we couldn't wait to dive back into full-time ministry. It's not that we couldn't function in those jobs; it's just that our hearts and dreams weren't in them. There's nothing else we'd rather do than what we're doing.

That defines for me my call to the ministry.

Knowing that this is what God has called me to do has kept me going when the church wasn't able to afford to pay me for my ministry. It's kept me going when my best singers called to say they weren't going to make it to rehearsal because they had other plans. It's kept me going when they didn't even bother to call.

Knowing that I'm in the field of ministry that God has called me to has kept me from hopping the fence when the grass on the other side looked greener. It's kept me going when those inevitable personality conflicts made me want to run to some other place of ministry or get out of ministry altogether.

Being called of God is a very personal thing, differing from individual to individual. I remember hearing my grandfather, a rough, rowdy oil worker turned Pentecostal preacher, tell how he stood in an Oklahoma oil field and heard God call him by name. My husband describes his call to the ministry as less dramatic but just as sure. And I've examined and confirmed my own call to ministry; it's not my grandfather's call or my husband's call—it's mine. It keeps me going on those days when I think about how nice it would be to just put in eight hours and go home.

"We are all called by God to share in His life and in His Kingdom. . . . If we find that place we will be happy. . . . For each one of us, there is only one thing necessary: to fulfill our own destiny, according to God's will, to be what God wants us to be."

—Thomas Merton

Are you called to be a minister of music? Search your heart, confirm your call, and then jump in with both feet. And never look back!

The Choir Pastor

The music minister is rarely the senior pastor of a congregation. But according to Calvin Johansson, associate professor of music at Evangel College, "The director must become a pastor to the choir." In other words, the first concern of the music minister should not be programs or learning new pieces or even the quality of music. According to Johansson, it's "the *people* in the music program."

If you consider yourself a musician but not a "people person," music ministry is going to be difficult for you. You'll find that most of the challenges that you will face as the music minister will not test your musical expertise or technical skill, but rather your ability to motivate and relate to ordinary (and sometimes ornery) human beings.

One senior pastor with whom I served told me my effectiveness would come from about 20 percent ability and education and about 80 percent skill in dealing with people. I've come to believe that may be an understatement.

"Relationships are both the professional and personal priority for pastors—getting along with people is an essential element of any ministry."

—Marshall Shelley

The minister of music—or any minister—must bring to his calling a sense of humility. If you take a church position thinking, "I'm going to educate these hicks and expose them to some real music," you are the one who is going to be educated and exposed, educated by being humbled—either by the congregation or by the Lord—and exposed as someone who cares more about showing off your musical expertise than serving your fellow travelers.

Johansson calls humble ministry "incarnational." That is, it reflects the humility God showed by reducing himself to man in the Incarnation. He says, "As a servant the music director is to wash humanity's feet, to minister to people where they are—not to lament the possibility of having to lower his station in life. . . . [The] pastoral duty of the musician is to care, to be concerned, to show regard for—in a word, to love."

I had occasion to speak at the annual music banquet for a large church. During the evening they honored one woman as Choir Member of the Year based on her faithfulness and perfect attendance record. Tears streamed down her cheeks as she told of struggling with an overwhelming alcohol addiction, even after she had begun to attend that church and joined the choir.

"Some nights I came to rehearsal drunk," she admitted. "I was ashamed, but I just felt I had to come anyway."

She credited the music minister's love and patience for helping her to solidify her walk with the Lord and eventually to stop drinking.

"This choir is all the family I have," she said.

I don't know what I would have done in that music minister's place. It must have been terribly awkward for him and his choir members. But they looked beyond this woman's thirst for alcohol and saw her thirst for God, for friends, and for love. That is incarnational love.

The Great Balancing Act

Ministry to the Lord, ministry to the body of Christ, ministry to our families, ministry to the unsaved—they're all pieces of the same puzzle. And sometimes, when we focus too narrowly on one piece, we lose sight of the overall picture.

But the Bible assures us that "we are God's workmanship, created in Christ Jesus to do good works, which God prepared in advance for us to do" (Ephesians 2:10, NIV). He views the pieces of our lives with eternal perspective and will help us fit them together to fulfill what He has called us to do.

One of the biggest challenges to any minister is that of juggling priorities. Sitting in a seminar, it's easy to make a list:

1. God
2. Family
3. Ministry

But putting it into practice is much harder.

For one thing, the lines between serving God, cherishing the family He gave me, and fulfilling His call to ministry often blur. Where does one start and the other end? All too frequently they overlap.

I haven't met a minister yet with all the answers. Most of us are constantly revising and renegotiating church schedules and family responsibilities, depending on the needs of the hour. For instance, when a new baby comes, for a while it seems the whole world revolves around that event. Other milestones in our lives (weddings, funerals, graduations, holidays) mean we have to do more juggling. Life is not stationary. Neither is a priority list.

Questions to Ask When Priorities Collide

1. Which program/obligation/event has eternal value?
2. Ten years from now, who will care if I was there? When ministry and family events conflict, who is more likely to remember your absence years later, your church or your family?
3. What does a trusted advisor or impartial third party say?
4. Am I doing this for the Lord or for myself?
5. What are my motives for choosing one priority over the other?

Take a Break

Being called into ministry doesn't mean there's no life outside of that ministry. In our ministerial balancing act, one of the things we are constantly juggling is time off. Dealing with people is exhausting. So is being creative, as every music minister knows. Without time off, those creative juices slow to a trickle. And even more important, in our era of the disintegrating family, it takes concentrated time and effort to nourish our relationships with our spouses, children, and extended family. They need to see more of us than the backs of our heads.

Whether you are married or single, whether you have toddlers or teenagers, you need a break from the music ministry.

- You need time off with your spouse to cultivate your marriage and to keep from growing apart. Don't make your partner take second place to endless paperwork, lack of preparation, or your own inefficiency.
- You need time with your family to get to know your children and to influence them by your words and actions. They don't need your reputation or your prestige. Instead, they need your example and your attention.
- And you need time for yourself. You need to get off the merry-go-round of rehearsals and services and take time to reflect on why you're doing all this and for whom.

Perhaps you're afraid to take time off. You have visions of returning from vacation only to sift through the wreckage of what was once a music program. But the fact is, no one is indispensable. (Not a real ego booster, but there it is.)

The choir really can limp along without their regular director for a couple of weeks. The accompanists will somehow manage to squeak by. Sure, the mail will pile up. But if you refuse to leave because there are still things left to do, you'll never take one minute off. Too many pastors and staff members let their ministries eat into their home life by coming into the office on days off "for just a couple of hours to get caught up." (I doubt whether there is such a thing as "caught up.")

"Beware of the barrenness of a busy life."

—Author Unknown

It takes discipline and organization to take regular time off. Prepare and train an assistant or layperson who can direct the choir in your absence. Or decide, along with your senior pastor, whether to dismiss the choir altogether during your vacation and feature guest musicians instead. Schedule accompanists and soloists well in advance, and reconfirm with them before you leave. If you're afraid the choir will forget you in two weeks, prepare a newsletter or memo to be sent to them in your absence. Then get out of town!

Consider this: Maybe your choir needs a break from you as much as you need a break from them. Just like kids who tune out Mom when they're with her day in and day out, your choir needs to see a new face and hear a new voice once in a while. Who knows? They might even appreciate you more when you come back.

Early Warning Signs of Music Minister Burnout

1. Your spouse is giving you subtle hints like taping a "Surf Hawaii" poster to the bathroom mirror or setting up the tent in the living room.
2. You keep taking your hands off the wheel to conduct the music on the car stereo.
3. Your kids recognize you only from behind.
4. You find yourself arranging the condiments in the refrigerator in rows according to height.
5. You make your family process into the dining room.
6. You start filling the candy jar on your desk with Rolaids.
7. You throw a tantrum during choir rehearsal—and no one notices.

Okay, so you're convinced of the need for rest and relaxation. But what about in between vacations, how do you make the most of those little islands of time in the sea of busyness?

1. Figure out which activities help you unwind and which add to your edginess.

Some music ministers want absolutely nothing to do with music during their time off. Others enjoy involvement in performance groups outside their church circle. One music minister friend likes to play his saxophone in the local university's jazz band. He says it keeps his skills honed and gives him a chance to play different styles of music than he otherwise would.

A ministry couple I know, who combine their music and drama backgrounds to direct the church musical productions, enjoy singing together in their community's civic light opera. It challenges them musically and, as they put it, "It's fun to perform without the headaches of being in charge."

2. As a family it's important to do things regularly, especially with children, to whom a week between Dad's or Mom's day off seems like a year, and a month of Christmas rehearsals is next to eternity.

Try to preserve at least one evening a week as your family night. Make popcorn, watch a family TV show or video, read aloud a chapter from a book or play the kids will enjoy, or if they're old enough, have everyone pick a role to read. Schedule a family outing one Saturday morning a month letting each family member have a turn at choosing where to go. In our family, the choices have ranged from the Natural History Museum (chosen by my son, the dinosaur buff), to Grandma's house, to miniature golf. What's important is to involve every member of the family and to have fun together. But write it down on your calendar, or it will never happen.

3. Sometimes church-related events, even those that are mandatory for the church staff, can be refreshing. If you must attend a church-sponsored retreat, instead of resenting it, go with the attitude of making it a time for personal reflection and prayer. If you attend one of the many annual Christian music conferences, try what one music minister friend does: He schedules a weekend off with his wife at the end of the conference. It's become a time that they both look forward to all year long.

The key is balance, that old juggling act. If you have a hobby that your spouse or children can't share, there may be seasons when you'll have to sacrifice some of your personal time for your family. Or your marriage may require some TLC, and you and your spouse will need to get a baby-sitter and go out together on a real date (and I don't mean grocery shopping). At still other times, you may find yourself needing to follow Christ's example and withdraw from those you serve to be alone with the Father.

Most churches and pastors recognize the need for paid vacations for their staff members. Many give a weekday off, realizing that Sunday is not a day of rest for ministers.

But sometimes a high-powered pastor, who verges on being a

workaholic, may be less than sympathetic to the personal and family needs of his assistants. The ideal time to find out is during the first interview for the staff position.

My husband and I were fortunate. Our first senior pastor was old enough and wise enough to regret not having taken more time out from his ministry to spend with his family, and he urged us both to take our days off. But we later discovered that all senior pastors are not created equal, and we learned to include the subject of vacation times and days off in our questions when we interviewed for other church staffs. Discuss it up front so that expectations—yours and the senior pastor's—are clear from the beginning.

Often as a church and a music program grow, the responsibilities and time pressures increase, too. When you suddenly find yourself at rehearsals, services, and meetings every night of the week, something has got to give. Then it's time to sit down with the senior pastor and try to reschedule the things that can be changed, and reevaluate the things that can't.

"Pastor, I have Joe here to see you. I think he has something to ask you."

Many churches are finding it necessary to formally set aside a family-at-home night each week when no church activities may be scheduled and families are encouraged to spend the evening together.

Approach your pastor with a team spirit. Be willing to cooperate with the other staff members and programs of the church. Learn to compromise graciously in dealing with who needs what personnel and facilities at which times. Offer to carry part of the load when someone else is on vacation. If you turn up your nose and say, "That's not in my portfolio," or you view all changes to the schedule as threats to the music department, don't expect a lot of sympathy to your pleas for time off.

What to Do If Your Pastor Won't Give You a Vacation

1. Come to the office dressed for the slopes. Be sure to stack your skis and poles in a prominent place, like near the coffeepot or on the secretary's desk.
2. Make a broken-baton-and-wire headgear (like the arrow-through-the-head) and wear it to a staff meeting.
3. Lapse into "musicalese," sprinkling your conversation with Italian phrases like, "Speak pianissimo, please. I have a marcato headache."
4. Whistle Handel's "Hallelujah Chorus" around the office. Involuntary listeners especially hate a lone harmony part. And if you can whistle through your teeth, so much the better.
5. Have a set of drums delivered to your office, explaining that you play them only when you need to unwind. Then proceed to play them all day. And start packing.

When the Going Gets Tough

Knowing you're called to a specific place for a specific time helps you to stay put when the going gets tough. And there's a lot to be said for staying in one place for a long time. Church growth studies confirm over and over again that the large growing churches have not only senior pastors but also staff members who have been there for several years.

It takes time for you to get to know the people you're ministering to and with and time for them to learn to trust you. It takes time to discover your areas of effective ministry and time to find out which programs reach the unsaved and which are just existing on life support because "we've always done it that way before."

And, as more than one minister has learned to his or her chagrin, if you run from a problem in one church, you'll most likely encounter it again in another church.

One music minister friend shakes his head regretfully at memories of his early career. "I did a lot of church-hopping when I first started in ministry. A lot of times all I was doing was jumping out of the frying pan and into the fire."

If we looked around for another place every time we became discouraged, the ministry would be one giant game of musical churches. Learn to let your call to ministry determine when and where you go, and don't give in to your feelings or circumstances.

"It is not success that God rewards, but always the faithfulness of doing His will."

—Author Unknown

Questions to Ask When I Want to Leave

1. Am I still called to this place of ministry?
2. If not, am I called somewhere else?
3. Am I running away from a problem here?
4. If yes, have I done everything I can, with God's help, to resolve the problem?
5. Would my leaving be good for the congregation I presently serve?
6. Would my leaving be good for my family?
7. Have I fasted and prayed for God's direction rather than reacting to my feelings?

♪

2

The Staff Member's Hat

Great Expectations

What's your stand on gambling?"

Hardly the sort of question we expected from the senior pastor, yet it was the first one he asked.

Afterwards, over lunch, the pastor said, "I guess you're wondering why I felt it necessary to ask you about gambling."

"Well," Ken admitted, "we were a little surprised."

The pastor explained that his former associate, the one whose job Ken was interviewing for, had seen fit to take some members of the youth group to Las Vegas (about a five-hour drive) for an overnight gambling spree. The pastor was on vacation at the time. You can imagine the welcoming committee that greeted him when he returned home!

After fourteen years of ministry, as both volunteers and paid staff as well as having survived something like two dozen ministry interviews, Ken and I have noticed something. We've observed that pastors reveal a great deal about themselves and the problems they've had with past staff members by the questions they ask during interviews.

One pastor friend always asks the spouse of a potential staff member, "Are *you* called to the ministry?" He's had a bad experience with a youth pastor whose wife hated the ministry and resented every moment her husband spent in it. Another pastor now tells staff applicants that he expects their spouses to attend church services, a statement he hadn't felt necessary until he had an associate pastor whose wife skipped services frequently.

If you've ever been on the receiving end of those kinds of questions, you probably felt a bit like someone tiptoeing through a mine field. You wanted to be both tactful and honest, but it was tempting to give answers you hoped would secure you a staff position.

There's a flip side, too. Those of us who've served in staff positions have also learned to ask questions of our own up front. The most important questions—from either side of the pastor's desk—are those that clarify expectations.

All of us, senior pastors and associates alike, come to a church staff with expectations: those preconceived notions about what it will be like, what we will do, how we will do it, and what kind of relationship we'll have with the other staff members. The problem is, expectations are often so taken for granted, so nebulous, that we aren't even aware of them ourselves, much less able to put them into words—that is, until we one day wake up, smell the coffee, and say, "It's not what I thought it would be."

The relationship between associates and senior pastors has a lot of parallels to the marriage relationship. What's more, it's the one human relationship (with the exception of marriage, of course) that will most influence and shape our ministries, now and in future positions. One way that the staff relationship most resembles marriage is in the area of expectations.

When a couple get married, they don't realize all the unspoken expectations they bring to the great state of matrimony. Take the dinner table, for example: If the bride's dad always helped fix the meal or set the table, she probably assumes her husband will be there in the kitchen with her without being asked. If the groom's mom routinely put the salt and pepper on the table at each meal, he is puzzled or perhaps even annoyed that his wife overlooked it.

Likewise, when a new associate joins a church staff, he assumes things will be like they were in his last church, or if he's new to the ministry, like he's imagined them to be.

Joe Youth Pastor's former pastor treated the staff as friends: He joined them for lunch and dropped by their offices to chat. Joe didn't realize he was expecting the same type of relationship with his new pastor until he got a memo directing that all conversation in the office be confined to church business.

Sue Music Minister was used to having a lot of freedom in her choices of Sunday anthems, seasonal musicals, and guest musicians. Her senior pastor was not musical and left that whole area up to her judgment. His attitude was, "You're the music expert. After all, that's why I hired you." Then Sue took a position with a different senior pastor, one who in his 105 years as a singing evangelist developed definite opinions about the kind of music people do and don't like and which guest musicians would set foot in his church. Sue was surprised by the extent of involvement the second pastor expected to have in her musical choices.

Unfortunately, most of our expectations aren't clear even to us until they've been disappointed. We don't recognize or give expression to them until we have a frame of reference, which comes only with experience.

That's why it's so important to try to identify our expectations before that first interview. It helps to talk to others in the ministry (both senior pastors and associates) about staff relationships and to get a feel for what it's like in greener pastures without having to jump the fence to find out.

One major area of differing expectations is the matter of time: How much time does the senior pastor expect of his new associates? This is especially tricky with part-timers who also work full-time secular jobs. Does he require strict office hours? If so, what are they? If not, how does he measure whether the associate is doing his fair share? What about days off? Vacations? Retreats? How many nights out per week are expected? Is the associate expected to attend every church function, whether it's in his department or another ministry? What about the spouse and family? What kind of time and ministry involvement are expected of them?

Other areas you might ask fellow ministers about are how much involvement the pastor (or pastor's wife, or board) has in his associates' areas of responsibility? To whom are staff pastors answerable? How much authority do they have to make decisions? Sue might have found out that her first pastor was atypical, that few senior pastors are that uninvolved in their church's music ministry. Or she might have discovered that some church infrastructures have whole music committees making the kind of decisions she was used to making alone.

Whether you find out things are better or worse on the other side of the fence—and chances are you'll find they're a little of both—it will give you a broader perspective and help you to identify some expectations you have about ministry. If nothing else, it'll help you come up with your own list of questions for an interview.

Coaches and Cheerleaders

The senior pastor is the coach of this team called the church staff. He sets the tone and defines the vision for that church's ministry. If he tends to compartmentalize his staff, discouraging communication between them, his associates will see their own departments as separate congregations. If he continually shares his vision for the church and emphasizes the goals shared by every department of the church, he encourages a team spirit.

The most productive church staffs I've served on were those where brainstorming was cultivated. You didn't have to be the Christian education director to have an idea about Sunday school or the music minister to suggest ways to promote the children's musical. That kind of sharing, coupled with respect for each staff member's ministry, gives us all a stake in every ministry of the church, not just our own. It discourages an attitude of territorialism, where we feel we have to protect our turf (budgets, lay personnel, activities), and keeps before each of us the big picture, overall ministry of the church.

"We need wide-angle lenses to view our place in God's broader plan for his church."

—Martha Nelson, Author

Joseph Linn, an arranger and long-time music minister, has said, "It's time to leave (your church position) when you can no longer be your pastor's cheerleader." By that he didn't mean that associates and pastors have to agree on everything. But we must share the same philosophy of ministry, the same attitudes, and the same major goals for the church body.

Linn recommends we make it an ongoing project to understand our pastors. This is sound advice, but it's challenging. It's so easy to evaluate those around us based on one or two incidents and then pigeonhole them as dictatorial, cold, unapproachable, or whatever label we've chosen. Yet we're all a mixture of conflicting personality traits, some admirable, some less so. Sometimes those of us in associate positions begin to resent the senior pastor's perks. He's certain to have a much bigger salary, drive a nicer car, and perhaps own a beautiful home. He's the one who gets all the respect and all the visibility. He's the one everyone turns to when they have a problem. Often even people we've worked closely with and know better than he does go to him.

But we need to remind ourselves of the other side of that coin. The guy out front is also the one who gets shot down first. It may seem that he gets all the respect, but he also catches most of the flak. And now that my husband and I have experienced pastoring a small church, I realize that most senior pastors have had to work their way up to the nice salaries, nice cars, and nice homes. Chances are they've been in churches so small they had to pay for bulletin covers and offering envelopes out of their own pocket. Few associates would think of doing that.

We associates also seldom ask ourselves, "Who pastors the pastor?" He gets discouraged and ill and has crises in his life, too. There are times when the pastor needs someone to minister to him. A caring, trusted associate can be that someone. We need to be as sensitive and supportive of him when he's under pressure as we wish he would be for us.

Keep the Trust

Like a marriage, the staff relationship has to be based on trust. When jealousy or distrust creeps in, the relationship sours. Once a trust has been betrayed, it takes a long time for the injured person to trust again.

For example, that pastor who asked us about gambling would most assuredly have had a hard time trusting that associate the next time he went on vacation. In fact, he probably had misgivings about trusting any youth pastor for quite a long time.

Trust is also important among associates. During a staff meeting, Jim, an associate pastor, made a comment about how he hated a particular song that the song leader often led. Imagine his embarrassment when a fellow staff member told the song leader about it. Jim assumed the comment wouldn't be repeated. The other staff member betrayed a trust, needlessly hurting the song leader, and opening a rift in the staff.

It's important for a pastoral staff to have the kind of relationship where they can speak freely among themselves and be secure that it will remain confidential. Just like any other profession that involves dealing with human beings, ministry has its share of frustrations. Staff meetings and conversations should be respected as opportunities for pastor and associates to voice frustration or other human emotions without fear of it becoming public.

A pastor's wife told me that gardening is her therapy. "I yank old Mrs. Grumbleglum out of my flower bed and shhaaaake the dirt off of her! Then I feel so much better."

Staff meetings are sort of like that. Sometimes we yank that choir critic or chronically late Sunday school teacher up and shake them around (figuratively, of course), and afterwards, we feel so much better. The associate who oversees bus ministry (whom we'll call George) might say something like, "Fred Fixit is driving me crazy. I keep asking him to check the brakes on bus five and he just won't listen! It's worse than talking to a brick wall—it's like talking to a radio because he talks back!" Then we all have a good laugh at poor old Fred's expense, and it helps George put those frustrations in perspective. Let me hasten to add that a staff that has the kind of trusting relationship that allows George to say something like that would also be able to gently remind him how far Fred Fixit has come in his Christian walk and how much George's patience has contributed to Fred's progress.

That kind of trust and mutual respect is the glue that holds a staff together. Without it there is no sense of being a team. Each staff member begins to feel he must protect his own backside (as Jim learned when his comments were repeated) and isolation sets in.

How to Betray a Pastor's Trust in Seven Easy Steps

1. Discuss disagreements between you and your pastor with members of the congregation.
2. Challenge his leadership publicly.
3. Spread abroad the news about who came to see him for counseling, what was said in the staff meeting, and other areas of confidentiality.
4. When you're thinking of leaving, let the pastor hear it from friends, other staff, or congregation members before he hears it from you.
5. When you have a confrontation with someone in the church, don't tell the pastor about it. Let him find out through the grapevine or, better still, in a board meeting.
6. Don't follow through on assignments or projects he asks you to do.
7. Take your youth choir to Las Vegas.

Handle with Prayer

It's vital for pastors and associates to pray together, not just over plans and programs but over personal and family needs as well. Praying together helps us to see our pastor and associates as more than departmental leaders. They are fellow travelers, battling with stress, juggling schedules, and dealing with half-hearted Christians. Praying together over more than just ministry needs helps us decompartmentalize our view of each other ("he's youth," "she's Christian ed.," "he's the senior pastor") and see ourselves as a team with the same goals and the same heart for the whole ministry of the church. Praying together helps us to be more compassionate and understanding of each other's shortcomings. It short-circuits jealousies and resentments that crop up among people who work together.

A close friend of ours, now a senior pastor, was a fellow staff member of mine and my husband's several years ago. During that time, he developed some health problems and he and his wife went through a frightening series of tests, diagnoses, prescriptions of potent medications, and adjustments to those prescriptions. While the rest of us on the staff knew he had had some sort of an illness, the senior pastor decided we did not need to know about its ongoing nature and told our friend and his wife not to discuss it with the staff or congregation.

As the doctors experimented with various types and levels of medication, our friend's behavior changed erratically. Often he dragged into the church office an hour after everyone else or left in the middle of the day. Sometimes he was irritable and even lost his temper on occasion. Those of us on staff began to pull back from him by avoiding him whenever possible and resenting what we saw as his slacking off. Finally, he and his wife invited Ken and me to lunch and explained what they'd been going through. It marked a turning point in our relationship; today they're among our dearest friends.

Had the senior pastor allowed them to share their fears and physical struggles with the staff, had he led his staff in prayer for them, what a difference it would have made! The rest of us would have had some degree of understanding and compassion for them. We could have reached out by helping carry some of the responsibilities instead of pulling away.

Consider the Criticism

No matter how good our relationship with someone is, it's hard to accept criticism. Somehow even so-called constructive criticism doesn't feel very constructive. Regardless of how it feels, it's what we do with criticism that counts.

Too often associates are not receptive to criticism from their pastors, and we music ministers are the worst! We tend to disdain criticism from a nonmusician. But we need to hear Lloyd Ogilvie, pastor of First Presbyterian Church in Hollywood:

"There is nothing more disconcerting to me than a director of music . . . who communicates in body language, facial expression, and sometimes words, that he or she is the only judge of what is appropriate and musically 'proper.' Just as no sane pastor would imply that a musician is not capable of evaluating what is effective in preaching, so too a sensitive musician should try to refrain from that impression about the pastor's knowledge of music."

Those words come from a pastor who ranks time spent with his music minister right after family and private study time. Whether or not you've been blessed with a pastor who puts that high a priority on his relationship with you, he's still your leader and his evaluation of the music ministry deserves your leader and his evaluation of the music ministry deserves your careful consideration. As one senior pastor is fond of telling his staff, "You're fishing out of my boat." Bear in mind that he is held ultimately responsible for all the departments and ministries of the church, so he has a stake in your music, too.

Admittedly, there are pastors who feel threatened by successful associates, and since music ministers tend to have more visibility than, say, Christian education directors, we can be more threatening. We're the ones up there in the spotlight directing the choir or receiving the bouquets after the Christmas production.

One acquaintance says his biggest problem is the "Saul-David Syndrome": a jealous senior pastor who is just waiting for him to fail. Still another set a record for longevity as music minister—a whopping two years—at a church where the pastor's wife felt she no longer had the time to direct the music program, yet couldn't bring herself to let anyone else do it. There's no easy way to serve in those kinds of circumstances, let alone accept criticism from someone you're sure doesn't want you to succeed.

Another particularly unwelcome type of criticism, used by a senior pastor with whom my husband served, is what Ken and I came to call the "shotgun approach." The pastor would assemble his staff and say something like, "It's been called to my attention that some members of the staff have been doing thus and so. . . . " Or, "Several people have mentioned that some of the pastors are too such and such. . . . " Inevitably the associates would look at one another in bewilderment, not sure if they had committed the crime or if one of their peers was the guilty party. They would call each other later and say, "Do you think he meant me?" I'm not sure if the senior pastor thought he was being kinder, but his indirect method only caused confusion and insecurity. Instead of changing or growing, the staff found themselves wondering who all these anonymous tipsters were.

I guess the moral of the story, if there is one, is to glean from criticism, constructive or otherwise, what there is to glean and try to let the rest go. Now, if I could only follow that advice. . . .

Conflicts in Staff Relations

When we boil it all down, there are only a few options open to us when we're having relationship problems.

The first option is to confront. By that I don't mean be confrontational, but rather go to the pastor or fellow staff member privately and try to resolve the problem. (Chapter 3 will outline some guidelines about when and how to confront.) I can't guarantee that it will patch up every troubled relationship. In fact, I've left two different senior pastors' offices knowing it had made no difference whatsoever. But it's the biblical thing to do, and I could live with myself better for having tried.

The second option is to stay put. From the statistics I've read and inquiries of my own, there seem to be quite a few ministers of music and other associates in this boat. In an informal survey of music ministers at a music conference, I asked them to name their most difficult people problem. Many complained about fellow staff members or senior pastors with comments like:

"Lack of spirituality and just plain integrity in the senior pastor and associates"

"Games played by the youth pastor"

"The pastor who is waiting for you to fail, watching for your mistakes"

"The pastor's lack of understanding about the work involved in the job of music ministry—'can't understand what you do all day long'"

I've said it before (see chapter 1) and I feel the urge to say it again: Know your calling. If you know God has called you to your place of ministry, and you know He hasn't released you from that calling, then stay put. And give Him your best while you're there: "Whatever you do, work at it with all your heart, as working for the Lord, not for men, since you know that you will receive an inheritance from the Lord as a reward. It is the Lord Christ you are serving" (Colossians 3:23–24).

The third option is to leave. We've already mentioned that if God calls you somewhere else or if you can no longer support your senior pastor, it's time to leave. Sometimes "having done all to stand" the rug gets yanked out from under you. You haven't sensed God releasing you from your place of ministry, but a pastor or board of elders have done it for you. Or perhaps the senior pastor has resigned, and your church's bylaws require you to tender your resignation as well. Or, as happened to my husband and me, you've gone into the senior pastor's office to let him know you're considering another place of ministry, and he's interpreted that to mean your two-week notice.

Regardless of what option you choose, or which is chosen for you, I want to encourage you: "We know that in all things God works for the good of those who love him, who have been called according to his purpose" (Romans 8:28). Ken and I have been through a couple of very difficult transitions between ministry positions, when we had to hang on to that Scripture verse for dear life. I truly believe that if we do everything we can to obey God's will for our lives, even if others act in conflict with God's will, He will work it out for our good.

Whatever option you choose, do it carefully and prayerfully. God will give you the grace—and that's a promise!

3

The Counselor's Hat

Fragile, Handle with Care

A few months into my first church position, having just fallen off the collegiate turnip truck, I determined I'd do more than just rehearse my adult choir—I would educate them. My professors had challenged us to be teachers as well as directors and to do more than just pound out voice parts. After some thought, I decided lesson number one would be about conducting. The choir would understand how to follow my direction better; besides, I didn't want these people to think I was just waving my arms around.

So during rehearsal we discussed $\frac{3}{4}$ and $\frac{4}{4}$ time; we practiced beating time together; we laughed and joked about who was catching on and who wasn't; we had a good time and everyone learned something. Or so I thought.

The next morning, Charlene, a soprano whose husband Gene was one of my best tenors, accosted me in the deserted sanctuary. "I want you to know that Gene went home totally humiliated last night. He'll probably never come back to choir again."

I was stunned, as though the wind had been knocked out of me. I tried to explain about wanting to teach them something to help them grow musically, but Charlene wasn't having any of it.

"We don't care how to beat time," she said. "We just watch your mouth anyway. But now, thanks to you, my husband feels too stupid to sing in the choir."

Fighting back tears, I asked if I could say or do anything to change Gene's mind.

"I doubt it," Charlene answered and walked away.

I sat there in an empty church feeling sorry for myself, my good intentions utterly misunderstood. I took Charlene's word for it that there was nothing I could say or do to make it right—so I never tried.

And Gene never came back to the choir during my term there.

As painful as that memory is, I review it for its lessons. Time and experience have allowed me to do that with some degree of distance, if not objectivity, so that remembering it now I hurt less for me and more for Gene. I regret that something I did or said, however well-intentioned, damaged another individual's self-esteem. I especially regret that I never told him that.

One of my biggest shocks about ministry has been the discovery of how fragile people are. Self-esteem is something most people work a lifetime to attain, and many never get a good grip on it. I've even observed that what appears to be boundless confidence in overachievers is really a thin veneer that is often brittle and easily shattered.

So many people struggle with a lot of emotional baggage. They remember the laughter of other thirteen-year-olds when their voices were changing and the tactlessness or impatience of music teachers who suggested, "Why don't you go out for track and field instead?" They're still listening to those parental voices in their heads that say, "You can't carry a tune in a bucket."

Over and over again I find that good, competent, talented singers in volunteer choirs have a much lower assessment of their musical abilities than I do.

"Do I have to sing in front of everybody?"

"Do I have to be able to read music?"

"You're not going to ask me to sing a solo are you?"

Their questions reflect their lack of confidence about their vocal and sight-reading skills.

Creating an Atmosphere of Acceptance

Most of us are music ministers because we love music and have achieved some degree of ability either by singing or by playing an instrument. Perhaps we've performed so often or been in the limelight so long that we no longer experience the "interior jellification" of stage fright. We've gained a modicum of confidence and have all but forgotten the dread of quavering or cracking on a note.

But for most people, nothing is more emotionally transparent than the voice. It reveals fear, fatigue, nervousness, anger, or joy—all involuntarily. Singing publicly makes us exposed and vulnerable, so to Joe Average, joining the church choir is an emotional risk. Our responsibility as music ministers is to create an atmosphere of acceptance and to make music ministry less of a risky business.

Jeanie, an enthusiastic new Christian, knew she couldn't carry a tune. The junior high chorus teacher and her mom had often told her so. But her heart was so full she just had to sing for the Lord, so she joined the choir anyway. Over twelve years later, when I came to Jeanie's church as music minister, it was hard to believe that this same woman who sang alto in the adult ensemble, performed solos and duets, and led singing for the women's group had ever been labeled "tone deaf." Jeanie attributes her musical growth to the acceptance and encouragement of her first choir director who, when he couldn't compliment her voice, praised her enthusiasm. He recognized that when you make people feel worthwhile, they'll do their best to grow into the role.

In church music ministry, particularly with volunteer musicians, we wrestle with the seemingly conflicting objectives of presenting to God our very best musical offering while accepting the efforts of those with less than perfect musical abilities. Cultivating excellence in music is a worthy goal, but it must not take precedence over the people who make the music.

Unfortunately, the same climate that cultivates musical excellence is also a hothouse for competitiveness, pride, and temperamental attitudes. Musical excellence should be one of our priorities, certainly. But it's not at the top of my list, and it shouldn't be at the top of yours.

In *A Circle of Quiet,* Madeleine L'Engle describes her struggle to breathe life into a lifeless choir in her Connecticut village church. After her first rehearsal with the tone deaf, the flat, and the one woman who "stayed in key, all right, but at full volume at all times, and with an unpleasant, nasal whine," she made up her mind that the problem voices would have to go.

"I couldn't do it," she wrote. "Something told me that every single person in that choir was more important than the music. 'But the music is going to be terrible,' I wailed to this invisible voice. 'That doesn't matter. That's not the reason for this choir.' I didn't ask what was, but struggled along. The extraordinary, lovely thing was that the music got to be pretty good, far better, I am now convinced, than it would have been if I'd put the music first and the people second."

When your choice is people versus performance, which do you choose? When we put the music above the musician, aren't we making the same mistake as those the apostle Paul said worshiped created things more than the Creator?

Several years ago at a music conference, I was privileged to hear Bill Gaither address this dilemma. Speaking to a group of church musicians he warned, "When you get to heaven, you're not going to be able to wave an Artist's Exemption Card at God. He's not going to be impressed when you say, 'I know I stepped on a few people but You'll have to excuse me. I'm a musician and You know how temperamental we are.'"

When we harangue choir members as people or as musicians, whether individually or as a group, we hurt the very people we're supposedly ministering to. What's more, trying to improve the musicianship by belittling the musicians is counterproductive.

I've been on the other side of the baton as a choir member whose director screamed and yelled and threw tantrums—and sheet music and chairs and other movable objects. I watched that professing Christian use his rapier to lacerate the self-esteem of young singers. Was the result a better musical product? Not at all. What he got was an us-against-him polarization of feelings within the group. Even if his scare tactics had improved the musical quality, a siege mentality set in that prevented ministry from taking place.

I've also been part of a secular group whose director nurtured mutual support and encouragement. Frequently he would select vocalists at random and say, "Sing us a few bars of something."

Warning Signs of Unresolved Conflicts

1. I resent choir-staff-family members for the demands they make on me, letting them control my time or emotional state.
2. My body is telling me things are out of balance through stress-related ailments: headaches, fatigue, high blood pressure, heart problems, ulcers, colitis.
3. I want to escape, to hibernate, and to stay under the covers.
4. I'm chronically angry, depressed, cynical, sarcastic, and I lash out at those I love.
5. My emotions fluctuate wildly.
6. I entertain thoughts of suicide.

If you can answer "true" to any of the above statements, it's time to reevaluate the problem relationship(s), whether it's at home, at church, or on the job. Seek help from your pastor or a trusted older colleague in ministry or a professional Christian counselor. Sometimes the stress is temporary—a particularly frantic holiday season, a financial burden; sometimes it is more fundamental—a tendency to take on other people's problems to a debilitating degree, an overwhelming need to please everyone. But finding another qualified person to talk to can greatly ease the stress and give you some perspective on resolving the relationship(s) or learning to live with it.

The others would listen appreciatively, applauding the unique style of each individual. Members were in direct competition with each other for slots in tour groups and opportunities to record and perform onstage, yet the atmosphere of acceptance and respect for each other's talent was sincere. It was made clear that nothing less was expected.

"People need people who believe in them, trust them, and expect much of them."

—Richard L. Evans

As the director, you set the climate control. If you've stepped into someone else's shoes in a new position, it'll take time to build an atmosphere of mutual trust. But you can begin by planting seeds of praise for the choir's, accompanists', and individual members' strengths. You can nurture an environment of acceptance by taking pride in the diversity of talents and musical styles within the church. You can encourage those with lesser talents by honoring their other contributions: faithful attendance, promptness, behind-the-scenes help with productions, robe maintenance, music filing, whatever you can sincerely find to praise. Set the example of enthusiasm, respect, and acceptance, and expect your choir to follow suit.

Confronting People

The challenge when dealing with people-related problems is to correct the problems without alienating the person. Remember, we never have the right to publicly embarrass someone in order to curb their undesirable behavior.

Jane, a new member of the church, was an accomplished singer and keyboard player and eager to join the choir. But with one car, three kids, and a chronically late husband who did not sing, getting to Sunday afternoon rehearsals on time was a struggle. One week Jane arrived late. She was frazzled by the efforts to get her uncooperative family ready on time, only to be greeted by the director in front of the whole choir with a sarcastic, "It's nice you could finally join us."

That director reacted out of frustration, something that all of us who try to begin rehearsals on time can relate to. But by giving in to her feelings and embarrassing Jane publicly, she nearly drove away a good choir member, one who eventually became one of her best accompanists. She should have spoken to Jane privately and learned the reason for the problem before assigning blame.

Another director I know faced an even touchier problem with two of her sopranos, a mother and a daughter. To put it bluntly, they had offensive body odor, and several other members of the section had threatened to quit if the director didn't do something about it.

Cara went to her senior pastor, and after discussing the situation, they agreed that she would have to talk to them. Gathering up her courage, Cara made an appointment to visit them in their home. As tactfully as she knew how she explained the problem, taking care to let them know how much she valued them as choir members. Their first reaction was hurt. Cara left fearing she'd lost them from the choir and the church. But a couple of rehearsals later, there they were having taken care of the problem, and now Cara says they're among her biggest supporters. She was honest with them, including being honest about her own discomfort at dealing with the situation. She was tactful and dealt with the situation in private, allowing them to maintain their dignity.

Some people problems are more subtle; some, more complex. A lot of psychological maneuvering goes on in relationships, even in the church.

A couple in my choir (let's call them Steve and Joyce) decided to join a church across town. They gave a general reason for the move to friends, but Joyce confided to me privately that the real reason for the move was to get away from the smothering influence of her in-laws who were also members of our church.

A few days later, Joyce's mother-in-law phoned me at home to ask what I knew about their move. I recited the standard story Steve and Joyce had been disseminating, but she persisted. "What else did Joyce tell you? She must have said more than that."

She alternated between pumping me for information and explaining in detail why her son and daughter-in-law had marital problems. After trying to sidestep her pointed questions, I finally said, "You really need to talk to Steve and Joyce about this."

"I knew it!" she said. "She told you they were leaving because of me, didn't she?"

I replied that I hadn't said that at all, only that it would be best for her to speak to them directly. She was intent upon catching me in the middle of a family dispute, and I was equally intent upon stepping out of it.

You must realize the possibility of being caught in a cross fire of this sort. In his book, *Games People Play,* Eric Berne describes a psychological game he calls "Let's You and Him Fight." In its most basic form, a woman gets two men to fight over her. There are several possible conclusions: (1) She may then choose the winner as worthy of her hand; (2) she may be attracted to the loser as the underdog who needs her; or

(3) while the two are fighting, she may walk off with a third man. Regardless of the outcome, she is in control, thus, the game is ultimately a power play.

Berne details many other such games and almost all of them are about power, about who's in control. Seasoned leaders become adept at recognizing the early warning signals that a casual conversation is developing into a power play. I've learned to trust my feelings when someone says something that makes me feel uncomfortable. Frequently the remark seems innocuous enough, but somehow, in some way I can't quite put my finger on, it just doesn't feel right. These mixed messages usually mean there's a psychological game going on; that funny feeling says, "Warning: manipulation ahead."

Staying Out of the Middle

You can take some steps to avoid getting caught between two opposing sides. Begin by learning how to recognize psychological games. When you know the speaker has an ax to grind, pay attention to where he's leading the conversation. If possible, steer the talk back to innocuous subjects, introduce someone else into the conversation, or excuse yourself and leave before the trap is sprung.

Pray for wisdom. Sometimes even the wisest minister finds himself caught between two sides and pressured to choose one.

Know where your loyalties lie. If the "Let's You and Him Fight" game involves the pastor or other staff members, choosing sides had better be a foregone conclusion. You have to be loyal to your pastor and fellow staff. And while I don't recommend speaking out in anger, I think it's appropriate to affirm the pastor or staff member's ministry to the critic, just as you hope would be done for you.

Encourage the two sides to talk face-to-face. Whether you take sides or remain objective, whether the two sides are pastor and parishioner, or daughter-in-law and mother-in-law, remind them that the scriptural way to resolve differences is face-to-face in private. "If your brother sins against you, go and show him his fault, just between the two of you'" (Matthew 18:15).

Staying Out of the Middle

1. Recognize psychological games.
2. Pray for wisdom.
3. Know where your loyalties lie.
4. Encourage face-to-face discussion.

Avoiding manipulation is sometimes enough. But when the unity of the choir is being threatened, it may be necessary to confront specific people.

Before you do, though, talk it over with the senior pastor. Chances are good that he's come up against this kind of problem before. He may have some insights for you, or he may be in on some confidential information that sheds some light on why the problem is happening in the first place.

Then pray about the situation. Hopefully you've already been praying about it. But pray some more, making sure that your motives are pure. Never confront another person with an attitude of revenge to even a score or set someone straight.

Examine yourself honestly. Are you by nature rash or impulsive? Does your temper or your words usually get you into hot water? Then think carefully about what you want to communicate and why it's necessary to confront this person. Ask the Lord to give you a spirit of love and concern for the other person.

If, on the other hand, you usually avoid conflict at any cost, you'll need all the power of the Holy Spirit available to you. Go forth boldly, address the problem head on—but in love, not anger or hurt.

"When attacked by a dragon, do not become one."

—Marshall Shelley

One of the touchiest situations I've had to deal with so far involved a confrontation with a senior pastor's daughter. Word came to me third- and fourth-hand that several of my sopranos were going to quit because they were tired of being the butt of jokes and sarcastic remarks by other section members. When I started asking for specifics, the "other section members" narrowed down to two people—the pastor's daughter and a friend of hers.

I swallowed real hard and went to my senior pastor with the problem. To his credit, he listened as impartially as a father possibly could, then gave me the go-ahead to talk with both of the offenders. I met with them separately and privately and explained the situation. Both took it pretty well. They said they hadn't realized they were hurting anyone and agreed to stop. The other sopranos were mollified and didn't quit.

In real life, which this was, problems you hoped were resolved have a way of cropping up again. As a writer I'd like to end this story "happily ever after," but as a colleague I'd be less than honest if I didn't tell you that even though that particular incident worked out well, others like it surfaced from time to time, usually involving the same people. Some people problems are like Paul's thorn in the flesh: always with us and never to be resolved. That's when you need the love of God, as described in 1 Corinthians 13, to keep loving people.

When You Must Confront

You will, no doubt, have to confront someone at one time or another. When you do, realize that timing is important. It's better to deal with conflicts before they magnify or fester, but *not* in the heat of anger.

Privacy is also necessary when confronting. If the other person makes it a public issue, say, "Let's talk about this in my office," or "I want to discuss this with you—would Thursday at three be a good time?"

Be sure you've thought through the problem and examined your own actions and motives. If you're wrong, ask for forgiveness. If you don't feel you're in the wrong, but you've still hurt someone (as I did in Gene's case), apologize for the hurt you've caused. (I should have.) Don't be afraid to share the blame.

Beginning with a positive statement is helpful. First, say something you sincerely like or appreciate about the person. (From educational psych you'll recognize this as a "sandwich" statement.) Then address the problem. Close with another positive statement letting the other person know you value him or her. (This makes the "sandwich" easier to swallow.)

Then allow the other person to present his side and really listen to him. Restate what you hear: "I hear you saying that you think I've been giving preferential treatment by using some soloists more than others." This makes you listen more carefully, lets the other person *know* you're listening, and allows him to clarify anything you've misunderstood.

Be specific. Point out a particular incident or statement that bothered you instead of saying, "I'm disturbed by your attitude." And differentiate between the behavior you don't like and the person you do like. "I really like having you in the ensemble, but it's hard to make the best use of everyone's time when you're half an hour late to rehearsals."

If someone verbally attacks or criticizes you, don't respond in kind. If you can't trust yourself to speak, stay quiet. It's easier to live with the regret of what you neglected to say than with the regret of what you did say.

When You Have to Confront

1. Realize that timing is important.
2. Understand that privacy is necessary.
3. Think through the problem.
4. Begin with a positive statement.
5. Listen to the other person.
6. Be specific.
7. Don't respond in kind.

Being Confronted

If confronting is difficult, it's even harder being confronted. When the "well-intentioned dragons" (as Marshall Shelley calls them in his book of the same name) spew forth fire and smoke, it's almost impossible not to get a little singed. But there are ways to keep from being consumed.

One of the hardest lessons to learn is how to let another person's anger roll off without taking it personally. My husband, Ken, is much better at this than I am, and his ability to listen calmly to an angry parishioner has diffused a lot of volatile situations.

In one church where Ken served as assistant pastor, a couple who supervised the junior Sunday school department asked to speak with him just before the Wednesday evening service. He agreed to meet with them briefly, after which he had other duties to attend to (making sure the various family night activities were running smoothly). An hour and a half later the couple finally finished breathing fire about a decision affecting their department, a decision made by the senior pastor and official board (and one which, unknown to the couple, Ken had advised against).

He could have reacted to their anger with angry words of his own. He could have shielded himself from the heat by telling them that he didn't agree with the decision either, providing them with fuel against the senior pastor. But he sat there letting them pour out their anger until it was spent. Ken was secure enough and had been in ministry long enough to realize that they weren't angry with him personally, but were frustrated that they had not been consulted about a decision that affected them.

Another tough lesson is sifting through criticism to really hear what's valid while ignoring the rest. One good gauge is if

"Thanks for letting me get that off my chest. I feel much better now."

the same criticism is coming from several sources. Another is whether the criticism is specific rather than general. And sometimes, like Ken did, you have to wade through the other person's pent-up frustration to find out what the real issue is.

"You're just like the last choir director—always playing favorites!" Lee complained loudly.

It was a good thing she was on the other end of a phone and not across the desk. I made a face at the wall. I'd been in the church only four months. I still didn't even know everybody's name, and she was accusing me of playing favorites! But, being the mature Christian I am, I calmly asked, "Why do you say that, Lee?"

She went on at length about how the same people always sang solos on Sunday morning, and because she wasn't part of that clique she never got asked to sing.

I have to admit I felt angry and defensive. I'd already been on staff at another church where I'd been constantly compared to my predecessor (and found wanting), so Lee had unknowingly touched a sore spot. But fortunately I'm not by nature a hot-tempered person, and except for grimacing at the wall, I didn't express any anger while talking with Lee. I mostly listened and then told her I had no intention of showing favoritism. I asked her to please give me a chance to prove it.

Time is a great gift when dealing with problem people: It not only heals the wounds they inflict but gives perspective and the increased ability to deal with other problem people. After Lee hung up the phone, time allowed me to hear that underneath the criticism: Lee was really asking to belong, to be accepted.

A sense of humor helps, too. Laughter has been described as the lubricant of life, and author William Ellis believes, "Humor can be used to patch up differences, apologize, say 'No,' criticize, gain cooperation, dissolve a hostile confrontation, and keep a small misunderstanding from escalating into a big deal." What music minister couldn't use a lubricant like that?

Psychologists and immunologists have joined forces in recent years to measure the effects of laughter on physical and mental health. While these gelatologists (researchers who study laughter) have yet to prove the long-term advantages of laughter, most are sold on its short-term benefits. Dr. William Fry, a Stanford Medical School psychiatrist and leading gelatologist, enumerates them: "Hearty laughter causes huffing and puffing similar to that resulting from exercise, speeds up heart rate, raises blood pressure, accelerates breathing, increases oxygen consumption, and gives the face muscles, shoulders, diaphragm (hear that, choir directors!) and abdomen a vigorous workout. As laughter subsides, there is a brief relaxation period, respiration and heart rate slow, often to below normal levels, blood pressure drops, and muscles relax."

"A cheerful heart is good medicine."

—Proverbs 17:22

This physical relaxation is just one way that laughter helps relieve stress. Another is the way laughing at ourselves punctures our pomposity, allowing us to step back for a moment and see ourselves—and our shortcomings and inconsistencies—honestly.

Ministry is somewhat like politics in that you or I can find ourselves praised and put upon a pedestal one minute and ambushed and put in our place the next. The ability to laugh at ourselves helps us keep our balance. It also disarms those who might be aiming barbs at us.

Abraham Lincoln, one of our best-loved politicians and perhaps one of the most astute, was known for his self-deprecating wit. When once accused during a debate of being "two-faced," he replied, "I'll leave that to the audience to judge—if I had two faces, do you honestly think that I would be wearing this one?" Ronald Reagan, whom frustrated reporters called the "Teflon president" because criticism failed to stick to him, was also a master at this kind of humor. It's hard not to like someone who can laugh at himself.

So here are some ways to put more laughter in your life:

1. Smile, laugh, be cheerful. You don't have to be a stand-up comic to see the funny side of things. Poke fun at yourself. Sometimes when I'm having trouble coordinating my conducting pattern to the music I use my left hand to correct my right hand. It's a way of saying to my choir, "Hey, folks, I haven't arrived yet." Don't confuse your sense of responsibility or dignity with taking yourself too seriously.

2. Spend time with family and friends, especially ministry colleagues, who laugh. Make a point of saving funny stories and

experiences for get-togethers. One ministry couple found it easier to survive the "troubled teen years" by asking their children each night at dinner, "Who can tell something funny that happened today?"

3. Collect things that make you laugh. Susan Seliger, author of *Stop Killing Yourself: Make Stress Work for You,* advises, "Make it a point to have on your bookshelf a couple of works that never fail to make you laugh out loud." Clip favorite cartoons and jokes, and include music-related ones in choir newsletters, on the rehearsal room bulletin board, or wherever it can do the most good. Listen to videos and tapes that make you laugh. (I highly recommend Bill Cosby for his humorous insights on family life.)

4. Be on the lookout for inside jokes in your family, on staff, and in your musical groups. Shared humor creates a sense of belonging and a feeling of togetherness like few other things can. If you have an annual event like a choir retreat or cast party after the Christmas musical, invite members to do a skit or a funny song. (I'll never forget one rendition by the entire tenor section of "Oh Lord, It's Hard to Be Humble When You're Perfect in Every Way!")

5. Try to look at even your most difficult problems with the eye of an observer. As Seliger says, "Try occasionally to look at even your most frightening problems with a distant observer's eye, seeking out like a detective, the smallest element that could be seen as amusing, silly, downright hilarious. . . . Once you can laugh, the pain and the anxiety usually diminish."

6. Remember that humor isn't always appropriate, and avoid laughter that hurts another person. Make sure your brand of humor is inclusive and makes people feel like they belong, not exclusive, which shuts them out.

Put More Laughter in Your Life

1. Smile, laugh, be cheerful.
2. Spend time with those who laugh.
3. Collect things that make you laugh.
4. Look for inside jokes.
5. Look for something amusing in difficulties.
6. However, remember that humor isn't always appropriate.

Perhaps the best advice I can pass along about ministering to people is that which Jesus gave to His disciples: "'I am sending you out like sheep among wolves. Therefore be as shrewd as snakes and as innocent as doves'" (Matthew 10:16).

Be shrewd, or "wise," as the King James Version puts it. Recognize the games people play; learn to avoid being trapped between warring factions in the church. Cultivate a healthy sense of humor that keeps the ups and downs of church relationships in balance.

But be innocent in your attitudes, motives, and actions. Knowing the psychological games doesn't mean playing them. Recognizing manipulation doesn't mean employing it. Laughing at incongruities (your own and those of your fellow pilgrims) doesn't mean using humor against others as a weapon of destruction.

Let the Chief Musician be your director; let the Wonderful Counselor be your guide. Confide your people problems and frustrations to Him. Bring Him the unresolved conflicts. Learn how to live in harmony with dissonant Christians. Then you'll never be afraid to face the music.

4

The Communicator's Hat

Have you ever stopped to think that the main business of the Christian is communication? Consider for a moment the three main reasons we Christians are here on earth:

- To worship and praise God (Hebrews 13:15)
- To become more like His Son, Jesus (Ephesians 4:13)
- To spread the gospel to all the earth (Matthew 28:19–20; Acts 1:8)

We humans slog through the muck of the mundane, experiencing fatigue, worry, stress, and try to worship an infinite, perfect God in spite of our finite imperfections. How we treasure those times when we break through to the spiritual realm and know we have been in the presence of Almighty God! But think how much better equipped and motivated we'll be to praise God when we are in heaven surrounded by His presence.

We struggle to be like Jesus, to put our "me first" attitudes aside and take on the mind of Christ. We grapple with the seeming contradiction between willing ourselves to be like Him and not relying on our own strength but the Spirit's. But won't we be changed into the image of Christ when we see Him? "Dear friends, now we are children of God, and what we will be has not yet been made known. But we know that when he appears, we shall be like him, for we shall see him as he is" (1 John 3:2). Think how easy it will be in heaven to be like Jesus!

When you think about it, there appears to be only one reason

we Christians are more earthly good than heavenly: We're here
to communicate the saving love of Christ to a world that doesn't
know Him.

Putting the Message First

Gospel literally translated means "good news." In fact, it's the
greatest news! But sometimes we music ministers can get so
busy polishing the vehicle—music—that we lose sight of the
message it carries, and if we can, so can our choirs.

When we put on the communicator's hat, one of our primary
responsibilities is to challenge our choir members, soloists, and
instrumentalists to put the message first. We must continually
hold up the message for them to see and say, "Remember, this is
what we're here for. This is what we're all about—not perfect
blend or flawless tone quality, as wonderful as those things
are."

And we must challenge them to do the same for us. After I've
worked hard ironing out the musical wrinkles, I need to hear
that bass close the rehearsal with the prayer, "Lord, help us to
remember that the most important thing we sing is Your name."

Sometimes we communicate the gospel not only *through* our
choir but also *to* our choir. People who don't have a close personal relationship with the Lord are often drawn to church music
programs. They come because they love music and want an
opportunity to sing or play. They see church music as a less
threatening way to get involved in music than, say, a civic
chorale or college choir. They also come because they're hungry,
but they often don't know what for.

Rick heard about his community's Singing Christmas Tree
from a fellow nightclub musician. He knew very little about
church, less about the Lord, but a great deal about music, so he
joined. As the weeks went by he recognized in others a peace
and purpose he'd never experienced. Sometime during that season Rick gave his heart to the Lord and eventually became one
of the adult choir directors in that church.

In our church we hold open auditions for our Living
Christmas Tree choir. Although some singers come from other
community churches, quite a few have no church affiliation at
all. Bill, who sang on the Tree our first two Christmas seasons,

told me recently that singing in the Tree choir had literally changed his life. "I didn't know what it was, but there was something different about the people from your church." At the same time a good friend of Bill's gave his heart to the Lord and told Bill about the peace he felt. Bill didn't join our church, but he did commit his life to the Lord and became deeply involved in a Bible-believing church.

Another woman who was already involved in a mainline church visited our Sunday morning service because of her participation in the Living Christmas Tree. That morning she responded to an invitation to give the Lord complete control of her life. She explained later, "I've struggled with wanting to control my life myself, but now I want the Lord to be in control. I want to have that kind of faith."

We need to be sensitive to those who come to our church or to our music programs who are hungry for the message we have. The Holy Spirit can give us discernment if we're walking in His power. And our section leaders or worship team members can help by being our prayer partners and by being ready to talk or pray with these individuals.

The Audience of Our Worship

The message is the "what for"; now let's look at the "who for."

Every now and then I ask my choir, "Who are you doing this for?" We need to ask ourselves, "Am I doing this to make Mom proud? Am I doing this to showcase my talent? Do I feel obligated to the choir director or pastor? Is this my ministry to the Lord and His body?"

Over and over we need to remind our choir, our worship team, our soloists, and our accompanists, "You are worship leaders."

Don Moen, composer and arranger for Integrity's Hosanna! Music, offers this advice to worship leaders: "Don't lead—worship." He's focusing on a truth we need to communicate to our worship team: To lead worship we must first be worshipers.

The place to start is inside. Am I a worshiper? Do I spend time every day out of public view and in God's presence?

From there I move to my worship team encouraging them to ask themselves the same questions.

Our next step is to worship together. We've recently begun to do that on a monthly basis. The singers and instrumentalists meet to go over some of our worship music for the next month, giving special attention to new choruses and the transitions from song to song or key to key. But the most important thing that we do is to just let worship happen by spending some time singing and playing for the Lord. We pray together by first sharing personal needs and then asking for God's anointing and direction over the worship services.

Pressed for time, we are often all business at rehearsals. But it is important to take occasional moments apart from working on blend or learning parts to read passages of Scripture on music and talk about the choir's role in worship.

When I learned that Skip, one of my best basses, had come back to the Lord years before through the ministry of the choir, I asked him to share his testimony in rehearsal. On another occasion, Jeanie, an alto, told what the choir had meant to her as a young Christian. Bob, one of our worship leaders, shared with the worship team how, as an unbeliever seeking to find God, he was drawn to those who worshiped God with hands upraised and faces shining with joy.

We music ministers hear words of appreciation for the choir's ministry more often than the choir members do. When parishioners say, "The choir music really blessed me this morning," or they write a note of thanks for a special production, pass it along to the choir. Words of appreciation and testimonies like Bob's, Jeanie's, or Skip's tell the musicians that they are affecting people's spiritual birth and growth. They need to know that they are truly communicating and ministering to people.

The choir, orchestra, and worship team members need to remember that their primary audience, more important than the congregation, is the Lord.

At the close of a long rehearsal, arranger and music minister O. D. Hall will often encourage his choir to sing an anthem they've been practicing "once more, with just the Lord as our audience." When the last note fades and there is that palpable sense that God has been listening, O. D. says, "Even if this is the only time we ever sing that song, it's worth it."

Encouraging Your Worship Leaders to Worship

1. Challenge and exhort them to *be worshipers* first and foremost, both privately and publicly.
2. Remind them that this is not a performance but an expression of the heart. The congregation is not their audience—God is.
3. At the same time don't be "superspiritual." Be real and transparent enough to admit that you don't always feel like worshiping, but you've learned that God's grace compensates.
4. Refer to them in print, prayer, and rehearsals as "ministers" and "worship leaders."
5. Set aside the music and look at the lyrics. Remind them again and again that they're conveying a message.
6. Encourage them to express worship in a way that directs other worshipers' attention to the Lord, not to themselves.
7. Pray together often for God's anointing on the pastor and worship team and for the Holy Spirit's direction during the services.
8. Minister to one another outside the worship services through prayer, fellowship, and help in times of illness or crisis.

Sharing the Vision for Music Ministry

Along with communicating the gospel message and encouraging the worship of God, we ministers must communicate our vision, goals, and plans.

The best way to motivate people is to share our vision for the music ministry, and let others make it their vision, too. Communicating this vision takes time and patience. One senior pastor with whom I served calls it bending twigs. He explains it this way: "If you want a tree limb to grow a certain direction, you start training it when it's just a twig. Each time you walk by, you gently bend the twig in the direction you want it to grow. Over time it will grow that way."

Another pastor sees it more as planting seeds. "I'll say to a congregation member or elder just in casual conversation, 'You know, I'm thinking maybe the church should consider so and so. . . . What do you think?' I listen to what the person has to say, even if it is the opposite of the direction I'm leaning, and let him know I respect his opinion. I've planted a seed. As time goes by, if I still feel it's a move we ought to consider, I may bring it up in midweek service, perhaps as an area for prayer. Again, I let people voice their views, or if it's not appropriate then I invite them to talk with me later. Eventually the idea will come up in an official board meeting. We'll take as much time as we need to examine all sides, then, if appropriate, make a proposal to the congregation. By that point nearly everyone has had a long time to get used to the change by mulling it over and even adding to or adjusting it."

Admittedly, this pastor has a wonderfully cooperative congregation and board, but he also recognizes and respects one important factor in dealing with human beings—we resist change. He's learned to give his people time to adjust to changes and to absorb his visions and attitudes.

You know people have made your vision theirs when they begin to say it themselves. Ask any member of Phoenix First Assembly of God what kind of church they belong to and they'll tell you theirs is a soul-winning church. Why? Because their pastor, Tommy Barnett, has been preaching it in the pulpit, in Sunday school, in staff meetings, and in the boardroom since he came to that church. And those people have really caught his vision!

Just as important as patience is enthusiasm. Be positive and upbeat about the church, the music ministry, and the future. Who wants to board a ship when the captain seems gloomy about the voyage? Not me!

Let your enthusiasm show in your face and your voice. If you're not by nature an outwardly expressive person, you may need to practice. John Plastow of Plastow Productions drama ministry gives the following tips for developing enthusiasm:

- Learn to smile more.
- Stand up straight.
- Walk faster.
- Speak quickly, clearly, and a little louder.
- Do everything as if you're doing it for the first time.
- Give yourself a pep talk.
- Know why you're doing what you're doing.

Ways You Can Share Your Vision

1. In one or two sentences define the purpose, the "reason-for-being," of your music ministry.
2. Regularly remind your choir and other music groups of their part in this purpose.
3. Decide who are the people with the most influence in your music department. Pastor John Maxwell, speaker and writer on leadership skills, says, "Twenty percent of the people have eighty percent of the influence." Find out who make up your twenty percent.
4. Ask the musicians frequently to pray with you for direction on how to effectively fulfill this purpose.
5. Mention major changes enough in advance for them to respond. ("I'm considering dividing the worship team into smaller groups. Any input on that?")
6. Listen to and respect their views. They may bring up an important point you might overlook. Even if you don't act on what they say, if you listen attentively, they'll feel they've been a part of the process.
7. Incorporate their suggested changes or additions whenever possible.
8. As your music ministry grows, include the directors of other groups, accompanists, worship leaders, section leaders, or choir officers in regular prayer and planning sessions.
9. Try not to be defensive about questions or hesitations regarding changes you propose. Often the resistance is just to the suddenness of a new idea, not to you personally. The less you wrap your ego up in your projects, the more flexible you can afford to be.
10. Be enthusiastic!

Encouraging Commitment

Ask any music minister—hey, *any* minister—what discourages him the most, and lack of commitment is sure to be up near the top of the list. Some pastors would even go so far as to say, "You just can't teach commitment." To that I would reply, "Maybe, *but* you can encourage commitment. You can nurture it, reward it, and hold it up as an inspiration to those you wish would emulate it." And maybe, just maybe, it would begin to spread.

Choir directors who stress proper breathing have choirs with better than average breath support. Music ministers who emphasize facial expression develop expressive choirs. If we want to cultivate commitment in our choir members, we must tell them, and keep telling them, how important it is.

Just talking about something doesn't make it happen, but it plants a seed (or bends a twig, if you prefer). When new members join the choir, orchestra, or worship team, make it clear that their faithful attendance is important not only to the director but to their fellow musicians. Let them know that their commitment is a high priority.

"The world crowns success, but God crowns faithfulness."

—Author Unknown

One way we can communicate that faithfulness is a priority is by rewarding it. When we tell our choir members we're more impressed by their dependability than by their talents, we've got to back it up. Few things cause more choir dissension and hard feelings than seeing those who show up for only the Christmas and Easter musicals get all the choice solos.

It's important to set minimum attendance requirements for all choir members, soloists or not, and be prepared to enforce them. Some directors rehearse each new anthem about six to eight weeks and require singers to be at no less than two-thirds of the rehearsals in order to sing it on Sunday. When tackling a musical, I have learned to hand out a schedule of all regular and extra rehearsals with attendance requirements in writing. Everyone understands from the start that if a singer misses too many rehearsals, he or she cannot sing in the performance. If you want to keep your options open in the case of illness or family problems, you can add something like, "At the director's discretion. . . ." However, beware of making too many exceptions or you will negate the whole purpose of encouraging faithfulness as well as open yourself up to accusations of favoritism.

Maybe those leaders are right who say you can't teach commitment. But whether it can be taught or not, it can be nurtured, stressed, and rewarded. It's important enough to communicate it in every possible way.

Encouraging a Family Feeling

All of us feel the need to belong to something, to identify with others. The music minister can cultivate a feeling of family among the members of the music department, and as it grows, among the members of each worship team or choral group.

Choir retreats, Christmas cast parties, and ice cream fellowships after rehearsals all contribute to camaraderie among choir members. But beyond that there are simpler ways to communicate to groups of separate individuals that they need to bind together. As Dan Crace has expressed it, "Choir members are more than just keys on an instrument. They are real people who face real life struggles and spiritual battles."

If Michelle's ten-month-old baby is facing surgery, let her share her fears with the rest of the choir and gather around her in prayer. If Don's wife will be bedridden for the next six weeks, send around a sign-up list for orchestra members to take meals to the home. When Beverly gets a job she requested prayer for last week, have her report it to the whole worship team.

"Be devoted to one another in brotherly love. Honor one another above yourselves. . . . Share with God's people who are in need. Practice hospitality. . . . Rejoice with those who rejoice; mourn with those who mourn. Live in harmony with one another."

Romans 12:10,13,15–16

As a choir or other musical group grows, members lose track of the new names and faces. Even in small groups, singers tend to get acquainted only with those in their own section. While visiting a megachurch during a convention, I observed in the choir room a large poster with a photograph of each choir member and his (or her) name neatly typed underneath. Shortly afterward I began posting names and photos of my own choir members. They loved it! It helped introduce them to each other and gave them a sense of belonging.

The discouraging thing about communicating—whether ministry goals and visions, commitment, the gospel message itself—is that there's always room for improvement. But another way to look at it is, there's always room to grow! As ministers, musicians, and *communicators,* we've got to keep growing, stretching, and taking risks. We've got to read everything we can, go to seminars, talk to other communicators, experiment with new ways of getting the gospel message across. Remember, it's the greatest news of all!

5

The Manager's Hat

So you're the new music minister. You arrive at the church office, unpack a few books, sit down at your desk, and then what? You haven't got the foggiest idea where to start.

"Whoa! Wait a minute!" You protest. "I should be so lucky! An office? A desk? A place to put my books?"

Some of you have the luxury of being confused in your own office in a full-time position. Others have to be confused with a couple of file cabinets in a Sunday school room and a part-time or even volunteer position.

But whether you're full-time, part-time, or volunteer, you need some organizational skills. In fact, if you're trying to juggle another job or homemaking responsibilities—which is another job, paycheck or no—you need organizational skills more than anyone!

"This year I'm going to get organized!" Every New Year's Day I make that resolution, but I doubt whether I'll ever have it all together. In fact, I'm beginning to think that it's impossible; I'm learning that for any of us, organizing our lives is an ongoing process as we grow and our needs evolve and change. But I take comfort in the fact that I am more organized this year than I was last year, or two years ago, or ten. And I keep resolving to be more organized next year!

In my attempts to get organized, I've discovered two major requirements: The first is to find the right tools for my particular needs; the second is to learn how to use them efficiently.

After that, organization is mostly a matter of maintenance, at least until my needs or those of my church require new tools.

This chapter will detail several of the organizational tools I've come up with myself or borrowed from other more organized people. I encourage you to adapt them for your church situation or use them as a starting point to create your own.

Determining Your Direction

They say that "If you don't know where you're going, any old road will get you there." The ubiquitous "they" also say, "If you aim at nothing, you'll surely hit it." While they are not always right, in the case of organizing and planning they have spoken the truth!

The first step toward organization is a step backward to look at the overall music ministry of the church. If you're new in music ministry, if you're new in a church position, or starting a new choir year, ask yourself these four questions:

1. What are my objectives for this music ministry?

Let's call objectives our general aims. All of us in music ministry share many objectives: to use music to enhance our worship of God; to reach out to the unsaved through the music; to edify the believer through "psalms and hymns and spiritual songs."

It's important to remind ourselves of these objectives regularly so we keep on track. Sometimes I think we should tie them on our hands and foreheads and write them on the door frames and gates like Israel did with God's commandments! If we don't have a reason or direction for all our organization, it's just so much busywork.

2. What specific goals will help me realize these objectives?

Goals are more precise than objectives. They can be measured: "I want to present a youth musical this summer"; "I want to see the choir increase by 25 percent this year." Make goals as specific as possible; they give you a yardstick to measure your progress. According to author Barbara Hemphill, "Research shows that less than 3 percent of the U.S. population put their goals in writing. It also shows that having written goals is high on the priority list of high achievers."

Set goals that are in keeping with your objectives. Ask yourself, "Is this goal (presenting a summer concert series) going to help me accomplish the objective (of communicating the gospel to unsaved people)?"

3. What musical events are expected of me by the pastor and congregation?

Unless you are pioneering a church (and perhaps even then), there will be expectations placed on you before you ever walk into the choir loft. If this church has always had a Christmas musical and an Easter musical, it's a sure bet that they expect you to continue that tradition. If the pastor has had success with a big fall music recruitment campaign, he'll want you to plan a music month in September. It's better to ask at the beginning instead of finding out in August.

4. What events would I like to add?

Perhaps one of your objectives is to encourage a greater degree of commitment in your choir members. One goal that would move you toward that objective is to reward faithful choir members by acknowledging them with choir awards. So you might decide to add a music department appreciation banquet in June before everyone leaves on vacation. Or perhaps a choir retreat would be nice in early September to get the fall music off to a good start. Maybe you'll decide to plan a special dedication service during music month to honor those who serve in the music ministry. Any or all of these events can help you reach your objective.

Keeping Track of Where You're Going

Most of the superorganized people I know are never out of arm's reach of their calendars. There's a very good reason for that. The busier you are, the more apt you are to forget what you're supposed to be busy doing and where you're supposed to be busy doing it and when and with whom.

So after you've listed those objectives, goals, and musical events, get out your calendar, a pencil, and an eraser.

Start penciling in your major events. Christmas and Easter are obviously first, then add others that apply to your situation. Will the choir and soloists provide special music for a missions convention? Don't forget annual events like a church anniversary celebration or homecoming, family Thanksgiving service, Mother's and Father's Days, patriotic holidays. Write down everything you know about or anticipate for the year.

While you're doing this long-range planning, count backward from a music event to where your starting points should be and pencil them in as well. (If the Christmas musical is on this date, then rehearsals should start by this date; music should be ordered by this date; I should start looking for a Christmas musical by this date.) Work backward from the event giving yourself a little extra time in case things take longer than you think.

Another thing to add to your calendar that many of us overlook is tuning of the sanctuary piano and any other church instruments requiring regular maintenance. Whether you're convinced it's necessary to tune the pianos once a year, twice a year, or at some other interval, pick a date and write it down.

Okay, you've looked at the overall picture and written in a skeleton plan for the year. Now it's time to start fleshing it out with some detailed planning.

Based on your answers to the questions in the previous section make a list of your daily, weekly, monthly, and annual tasks. Assign a day or time for each one. Some are already decided for you, like a weekly staff meeting every Tuesday morning, or adult choir rehearsal every Wednesday night. Write those down and then plan around them.

Perhaps you'll want to make Tuesday afternoon your rehearsal-planning time. Have both a long-range plan ("Eight to ten Sundays from now I want the choir to sing this new anthem") and a weekly plan that moves toward it ("I'll introduce it with one brief run-through this week"; "I'll spend ten minutes going over parts next week," etc.)

Maybe you'll decide that the third Tuesday of each month is your time to plan the worship music for the following month. Decide whether you'll introduce new choruses to the congregation by using them as offertories, instrumental preludes, or by having the choir sing them first as an anthem or call to worship. This is your time to plan worship and choir music that fit together. If the pastor is preaching a sermon series or through a certain book of the Bible, ask if he knows what his texts or subjects will be for the month, and plan music that reinforces those themes.

If you use instrumentalists who play other than C instruments, planning is a must! Although some musicians are accomplished enough to transpose on sight, it's really presuming a lot to wait until service time to inform them of the congregational music. Because our church has several instrumentalists who need music transposed to their key, our worship leaders know that they can't just throw something together at the last minute.

If you are the one who arranges and transposes the instrumental accompaniment parts, set aside a regular day and time for that, too. One music minister friend, who does a great deal of arranging, sets aside every Thursday and is unavailable for phone calls or meetings on that day, except in emergencies.

Listening to new music is one of my problem areas, probably because it involves making decisions that I'd rather postpone. The only way to deal with the mountain of accumulated music from music publishers' choral clubs and music conferences is to make an appointment with myself at least one day a month. But first, I find it helps to make a list of music I'm looking for: Communion songs, children's Mother's Day songs, lively opening choral anthems. This lifts the load of decision-making a little by narrowing down my music needs. The limits of the music budget and rehearsal time are also effective in narrowing down choices of music I like but can't afford or don't have time to teach in rehearsal.

Are you responsible for scheduling solos, duets, and trios for the worship services? Make a list of all the soloists and groups in your congregation, pick a date to sit down with your master calendar, and schedule a month at a time. After you get the glitches worked out of it (like remembering to plan around Robin who is in children's church every other Sunday morning, and Joe who has to work the first Sunday night of the month), try scheduling a quarter (three months) at a time. Type up the list, photocopy it, and distribute it to every singer and instrumentalist involved. You can always make changes in your plan if someone is ill or out of town. But a soloist, for example, having a list with her name on it gives her a goal to work toward. I've found it's much more effective than saying, "I'd like you to prepare a solo; let me know when you're ready to sing it."

Managing the Paper Piles

There's always more paperwork than a new music minister expects. And as the ministry grows, so does the volume of mail, music, rehearsal schedules, and publicity layouts. Paperwork is a lot like housework—it's frequently drudgery, but it's easier if you keep on top of it rather than let it pile up.

"I'm going to work at home. It's too noisy in my office!"

Barbara Hemphill, in her book *Taming the Paper Tiger,* says, "Paper clutter is postponed decisions; paper management is decision making." Look at your desk, briefcase, or workspace. Do you see a lot of postponed decisions staring back at you?

> *"If you don't know you have it, or you can't find it, it is of no value to you."*
>
> —Barbara Hemphill

The superorganized say you should handle a piece of paper only once. While that is probably impossible for most of us, think about those papers you've been carrying around in your briefcase or shuffling into piles on your desk. How many times have you picked them up and looked through them, only to replace them without taking any action?

Hemphill suggests seven places to put paperwork:

1. "To Sort" Tray. When you really don't have time to act on the paper, you put it here, but you make an appointment to go through this tray regularly. (This would be a good item to mark on your weekly calendar.)

2. "To Do" List. You should keep this list, along with your calendar, with you at all times. Leave space to number the items on your "To Do" list in order of priority. Hemphill also suggests putting like items together on the list, for example, calls you need to make or errands you need to run, so that you can make the best use of your time.

3. Calendar. Is the paper you're holding notifying you of an upcoming event you're interested in? Pencil it in on your calendar, along with deadlines for registering (put a note on those dates, too), phone number to call, and any other necessary information.

4. Rolodex or Phone Book. If the only reason to keep the paper is for a phone number or address, transfer that information to your Rolodex or phone book and then toss the paper.

5. Wastebasket. The "art of wastebasketry," according to Hemphill, is "one of the most essential skills to learn and use

for effective paper management." When handling a piece of paper ask yourself, "Do I really need this?" If you can record the information in your Rolodex, calendar, or "To Do" list, or if the paper is for your information, and now you know it—throw it away!

6. Action Files. These are for current projects, perhaps the musical you're planning now or the upcoming music department banquet. I've recently begun carrying a large three-ring binder that serves as my "action files." Because I also use it for music, and because I don't usually carry a briefcase, I find it more flexible than file folders.

7. Reference Files. You've considered all the other options for this piece of paper—the "To Do" list, the calendar, the Rolodex, the wastebasket, and the action files—and you still need a place to keep it. This is a job for "reference files." But keep your filing system simple, or you'll never be able to find that piece of paper again.

Add all the normal office paper clutter to the stacks of octavos, chorus sheets, and musicals a church music program uses each week, and you can feel buried in paper.

I remember feeling overwhelmed when I accepted the music minister's position of one large church. One look at the extensive music library told me that this choir had done many of the recent major musicals, and I wondered how I would ever get up to speed. I began by asking the interim choir director, a layman in the choir, to make me a list of the choir's best-known (and best-loved) songs and anthems. His list proved invaluable in those first few weeks as I rehearsed the choir for each Sunday's music, trying to become acquainted with each of them as well as the contents of the music library.

The second thing I did was begin a card file. I tried to set aside time each week to go through every piece of music: sorting, cataloging, counting, sometimes giving away, and even throwing away the really outdated octavos. All the photocopied music went into the wastebasket, except one sample copy of each song, while I tried to locate ordering information. (If a piece is no longer in print but is still worth singing, write to the publisher and ask for permission to photocopy it.)

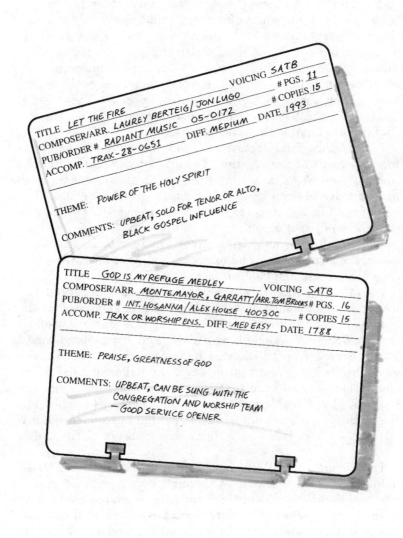

TITLE _LET THE FIRE_   VOICING _SATB_
COMPOSER/ARR. _LAUREY BERTEIG / JON LUGO_   # PGS. _11_
PUB/ORDER # _RADIANT MUSIC   05-0172_   # COPIES _15_
ACCOMP. _TRAX-28-0651_   DIFF. _MEDIUM_   DATE _1993_

THEME: _POWER OF THE HOLY SPIRIT_

COMMENTS: _UPBEAT, SOLO FOR TENOR OR ALTO,_
       BLACK GOSPEL INFLUENCE

TITLE _GOD IS MY REFUGE MEDLEY_   VOICING _SATB_
COMPOSER/ARR. _MONTEMAYOR, GARRATT / ARR. TOM BROOKS_ # PGS. _16_
PUB/ORDER # _INT. HOSANNA / ALEX HOUSE   40030C_   # COPIES _15_
ACCOMP. _TRAX OR WORSHIP ENS._ DIFF. _MED EASY_ DATE _1788_

THEME: _PRAISE, GREATNESS OF GOD_

COMMENTS: _UPBEAT, CAN BE SUNG WITH THE_
       CONGREGATION AND WORSHIP TEAM
       — GOOD SERVICE OPENER

Those cards became my music inventory and more. I bought a Rolodex card file with four- by six-inch size cards. (A card file box will work, too.) On each card I listed the title, composer, publisher, ordering number, and number of copies in the file. Just as important, I wrote comments that really saved time when searching for just the right piece of music later: "Upbeat—good choral opener"; "Soft, worshipful—use for Communion or Easter season"; "Youth ensemble, appropriate for Thanksgiving season—Jennifer does first verse solo." I also cross-referenced the cards with separate categories for each musical group in the church, for seasonal categories, and for themes like "Communion," "Missions," and "Patriotic." My successor in that ministry position later told me he used the card file extensively while he was getting acquainted with the church's music program.

Instead of a card file you might want to put your church's music inventory on computer. You'll still have to type the information to store it in the computer, just as you would on cards. But if the program you use has a quick retrieval system, alphabetizes for you, and can cross-reference, it could save you time when you're looking for that certain piece of music to fit the pastor's sermon series. Items to consider before going with a computer program instead of a card file:

- Does the church have a computer and a program that will meet my music inventory needs?
- If so, will I have ready access to the computer, or will I have to schedule my time on it?
- Will others who will need to use the music file (directors of other music groups, secretaries, volunteer helpers, my successor) be able to use the computer file?

If you're not sure which is better, do some research. Ask other music ministers how they catalog their music. If they use a computer program, ask for some training before you spend money on a program. If you decide to go with a computer file, don't do a card file, too. It will just double your time and effort.

But what about the music itself? For storing octavos, file folders and drawers are fine. The folder tabs should be clearly marked by the song title and filed alphabetically. For books (musicals and song collections) I recommend a method used by one music minister. She uses boxes designed for storing music books and glues a photocopy of the book's title page on the outside binder of the box. This is an easy way to list the title, the composer-arranger, and the table of contents and have it all available at a glance.

Tips for Your Reference Files

- When you think of the information you plan to file, what is the first word that comes to mind? File it under that word.
- Always file in alphabetical order.
- File information according to how you will use it, not where it came from. For example, you get a music publisher's newsletter with a great article on using drama in musicals. The next time you're planning a musical, you're more likely to look for it under "Drama" than under the publisher's name.
- Put papers in a general file category first, for example, "Christmas." Then if the file becomes too bulky, break it down, for example, "Christmas: Children," "Christmas: Costumes," etc. But remember, it's easier to look through one file with twenty pieces of paper than ten files with two pieces of paper in each.
- Keep a file index listing the file names alphabetically in the front of the filing system or at your desk. This helps not only *you* remember how you labeled something, but anyone who might help with your filing (not to mention your successor).
- If you don't have the luxury of your own secretary, make a weekly appointment on your calendar to do your filing.
- One of the main reasons people resist filing (beyond the anxiety of deciding where something goes) is that they hate jamming their hands into overstuffed file drawers. So clean out the files as you use them. When you see an unnecessary piece of paper in the file, instead of putting it back with a

sigh and a "Someday . . ."—toss it right then. Hemphill advises making an annual "File Clean Out Day." A good time for the music minister might be around annual report time or just after Christmas.

What to Keep in an Action Files Notebook

1. Calendar
2. Phone book or membership list of adult choir or other music groups and congregation members
3. "To Do" list, blank paper
4. Current rehearsal schedules, worship music schedules
5. Music currently being rehearsed by adult choir (with holes punched in it to secure it in binder)
6. Tabbed dividers to separate different projects or music groups (e.g., Living Christmas Tree, Children's Choir, worship music)
7. Current project notes, script, music: Christmas, Easter, etc.
8. Postcards, notes, and stamps for jotting quick reminders, thank-yous, or follow-up notes to absentees
9. Clear vinyl sheet protectors, the top-loading kind with three holes already punched in them, for pages I don't want to punch holes in, for example, clip art or masters for photocopying (these sheets are also handy for carrying small items like cassette tapes, pencils, and postcards)
10. Choruses or lead sheets, plus blank manuscript paper for arranging instrumental parts for the worship services

---

Planning the Rehearsals

We've all seen the bumper sticker that reads "Plan ahead," with the first several letters evenly spaced and the last letters all scrunched together where the writer ran out of room. That's pretty similar to what happens in a choir rehearsal that hasn't been planned.

I find that the time and care I take in planning rehearsals frees me to conduct with more confidence rather than drifting haphazardly from one song to another. And knowing where I'm going and what I want to accomplish eliminates a lot of the frustration busy choir members feel when they suspect their time is being misspent.

Studies on learning and memory show that we learn better

and retain more of what we learn when we study it in shorter intervals over a longer span of time. By planning your choir music at least eight to ten weeks ahead, you can afford to spend less time on each song per rehearsal by reviewing it over more weeks. It's a struggle getting to the point where you're working eight weeks ahead, but once you're there it's just a matter of replacing the songs just sung with new ones each week.

Some other ways to pick up the rehearsal pace:

1. Give choir members, accompanists, sound technicians—everyone involved in the rehearsal—their own copy of a written rehearsal schedule. Tailor it to your own situation with instructions regarding instrumental or taped accompaniments. This allows singers, instrumentalists, and technical personnel the opportunity to get their music and tapes in the proper order at the beginning of rehearsal. It also gives them a sense of accomplishment; they can see their time isn't being wasted. And knowing how much music is left to learn cuts down on visiting between numbers.

2. Schedule around any delays you can reasonably anticipate: changing or cuing accompaniment tapes, tuning instruments. Through the campaigning of my sound guys, I finally learned not to schedule two different reel-to-reel numbers next to each other in rehearsal. It takes time to rewind one reel, take it off, and replace the next. This is time that you could use rehearsing a song with piano accompaniment. Now reel-to-reels have become obsolete and CDs can locate any place in the music instantly.

3. Always maintain control of the rehearsal by projecting an attitude of cheerful confidence and organization. Keep the pace brisk and challenging.

4. Receive the messages, verbal and nonverbal, that your choir is sending you. Are they bored or restless? Maybe they're not being challenged. Are they frustrated? Maybe they feel their time is being wasted in rehearsal. If you're not sure, ask someone in choir you trust, or give the choir periodic questionnaires to fill out anonymously, inviting positive suggestions for change. And don't react defensively. Be secure enough to consider their comments as expressions of their needs instead of as personal criticisms.

Suggested Choir Rehearsal Schedule

Rehearsal Music:
Date:_____

_____	Cass.___	CD___	Piano___	Organ___	Synth.
_____	Cass.___	CD___	Piano___	Organ___	Synth.
_____	Cass.___	CD___	Piano___	Organ___	Synth.
_____	Cass.___	CD___	Piano___	Organ___	Synth.
___·_____	Cass.___	CD___	Piano___	Organ___	Synth.
_____	Cass.___	CD___	Piano___	Organ___	Synth.
_____	Cass.___	CD___	Piano___	Organ___	Synth.
_____	Cass.___	CD___	Piano___	Organ___	Synth.
_____	Cass.___	CD___	Piano___	Organ___	Synth.

Special Instructions: _____
Announcements: _____
Prayer Requests: _____
Sunday Morning Choir Songs: _____
Sunday Evening Choir Songs: _____

Adventures in Budgeting

I remember well the first time my senior pastor asked me to prepare a music budget for the church board's consideration. I thrashed around for a couple of days like a fish in a boat looking for an escape. Finally, time was running out and I had no choice but to do something! It turned out to be a tedious task but not nearly so painful as I'd feared.

I started by finding out how much money had been spent on the music program in the past year. I was lucky that the church had an organized, itemized bookkeeping system, which allowed me to categorize the areas of spending instead of just writing down a lump sum and labeling it "Music."

I went through the checkbook ledger for the previous twelve months listing amounts spent for anything that came under the umbrella of the music department: music for the children's choir, spotlight rentals, postcards for absentee choir members, newspaper ads for the Christmas musical, everything. After making a list, categorizing the amounts spent, I tried to project what expenses I would need to add in the coming year.

That first budget was hard to get started, but I survived and so will you. Try thinking of it as an adventure, a challenge to do the very best with the resources available to you. Recognize that the bottom line can be a helpful tool in persuading cautious board members that what you want is really in the church's best interests. For example, one year I drew up a comparison for the board showing them what the church was currently spending each year on spotlight rentals and what it would cost to buy two spots of our own. After they saw that the lights would pay for themselves in two years, the board approved the purchase.

Use your budget as a stimulus to setting priorities in your music ministry, to putting first things first.

Things to Think about When Working on a Budget

1. Music minister's salary and expenses, if these are considered part of the music budget
2. Music (include Christmas, Easter, other special musical events, age-level groups, estimated new pieces for regular worship services, instrumental, accompaniment tapes or CDs, rehearsal tapes)
3. Costumes, props, scenery
4. Lighting and sound equipment rental or purchase
5. Publicity: printing and postage costs, typesetting, advertisements
6. Child care for rehearsals
7. Music conventions, workshops
8. Choral clubs, church music periodicals
9. Awards or gift certificates for accompanists, assistants
10. Maintenance of instruments
11. Cleaning or replacing robes
12. Special items: new hymnals, new folders for worship music, dissolve units and projectors for multimedia productions—think big here!

When you look around your office or workspace evaluating your organizational skills (or lack thereof), remind yourself that we're all "in process." None of us have arrived yet. Rather than flagellating yourself for not having it all together, determine to improve just one thing about your ministry management this month. Use some of the ideas here, adapt them to your needs, making a change you can live with. Then next month, try another organizational tool or create one yourself.

The important thing is to keep "pressing toward the mark" by striving for excellence—not measuring our success by the world's standards but by our effectiveness as God's ministers.

6

The Talent Agent's Hat

Equipping the Saints

How's the new music minister working out?"

"Well," came the sarcastic reply, "He's got the choir whittled down to a manageable size."

And so it goes for the leader who is not willing to recruit and train volunteers. He or she will never have a group larger than one person can manage.

There are lots of other reasons to recruit. None of us can do everything, much less do it all well. Helpers multiply our hands, our eyes, our voice. Perhaps more important, the call to ministry includes a call to "equip the saints" for ministry. If we don't provide places and means for people to serve, we are robbing them of ministry in the Lord's church; we're amputating parts of His body or not allowing them to grow and develop in the first place. That is, the Church, local and universal, is a living organism, a community of believers working and worshiping together. The apostle Paul used the analogy of each individual as a member of the body with its own specific function. How many of us can afford to lose body parts?

"Alone I cannot serve the Lord effectively, and He will spare no pains to teach me this. He will bring things to an end, allowing doors to close and leaving me ineffectively knocking my head against a blank wall until I realize that I need the help of the Body as well as of the Lord."

—Watchman Nee

78

How do we help others discover their function in the Body? There's no formula or equation when you're dealing with human beings, but there are a few qualities good talent agents share.

First, communication. Share not only your "holes that need filling" but also your goals and visions for the music department and how others can help you reach them. Include them in your goals and allow them to add to or refine your plans until they begin to make your vision their own.

Communicate the needs of the music ministry through every means available to you: music brochures, bulletin and pulpit announcements, church mailing lists, newsletters, calendars, and even follow-up of new visitors.

Jane, a music director for a large church, makes it a point to meet visitors each Wednesday evening at the church fellowship dinners. One way that church welcomes newcomers is by offering them their first Wednesday dinner free of charge. Jane seeks these folks out, introduces herself, and asks them if they are musical or interested in knowing more about the music program. She's very good at it, too. Her music department boasts more groups and directors than many churches triple the size.

Another quality that makes Jane such a great recruiter is her lack of professional jealousy. She's not afraid of using someone with greater technical skill or a longer string of music degrees for fear they'll upstage her. In fact, she's pleased to have them and has built a varied music program around the strengths of many talented people, instead of arranging it to revolve around herself.

Not that it's always easy. All of us have our own areas of insecurity, try as we might to hide or overcome them. Perhaps the insecurity is in an area of weakness, and to accept help would be an admission of inadequacy.

But for me, I think jealousy or insecurity is more likely to rear its ugly head in my areas of strength, where I don't feel I need help. For example, I do not feel confident in some of the technical matters like staging or blocking a production or designing sets or lighting. Consequently, I have no trouble asking someone with more expertise to handle those tasks for me. But I do consider myself a trained vocalist and a good conductor. I'm more apt to feel threatened by someone with a string of degrees in voice training or conducting than by someone with a theater and drama background.

Regardless of what inhibits or threatens me, I have to get beyond that insecurity. Once again, it helps to remind myself of my calling, to be secure in knowing this is where God has put me for this time. Then I can look past my needs and at the other person's need to be involved in ministry. And I keep praying that God will make me the kind of leader who is big enough to rejoice in the strengths and talents of others and not so small that I can't allow others to succeed.

Finding Potential Leaders

When looking for other leaders, it's important to listen to the ideas and conversations of people around you. Do they express dreams and goals?

Jane began to watch a young mother in her congregation, Carolyn, whose take-charge organizational ability stood out. Carolyn's faithfulness to the women's ensemble in spite of three young children also impressed Jane, who asked her to direct the children's choir. Five years later, the same creative and organizational skills that made Carolyn a good children's director were put to use coordinating the Singing Christmas Tree program at that church.

"Make all, within your society, members of the crew and permit no passengers."

—Elton Trueblood

Perhaps the two most important qualities to look for in potential leaders are dependability and teachability. I certainly believe such qualities are far more important than musical skill or experience.

Shannon was an extremely talented pianist, one of the best I've ever known. She could play any kind of music—classical, southern gospel, and everything in-between—with or without a score. But she was a "floater." She floated in and out of our church and our music program two or three times in a half-dozen years, never sticking for more than a few months at a time. Was she a nice person? Sure. Talented? Without a doubt. Was she an asset to our music ministry? No. We never knew if she'd be there or not.

Watch people you are considering for leadership. Those who are responsible in one area tend to be responsible in other areas as well. Is he on time? Does she often call at the last moment and cancel? Does he carry through on a project or abandon it half-done?

Look for the quality of teachability also. How does a potential leader respond to your suggestions? Does he automatically dismiss them, or does he stop to consider your point of view? A person with limited talent or experience but with an eagerness to learn is eminently more qualified for leadership than someone who thinks he knows everything already and thus has nothing left to learn.

Some Ways You Can Recruit People

1. Music brochure. Design one describing activities and requirements of each music group. Include the brochure in the visitors packets for each service.
2. Personal contacts. Call or meet newcomers personally. Search them out at church social functions and before and after services.
3. Music surveys and questionnaires. Include these periodically in the church bulletin or mailer on a quarterly or semiannual basis.
4. Music recruitment programs. Develop your own theme, or check into professionally done membership drive programs.
5. Music teachers and schools. Talk to teachers in the congregation or call local schools and colleges, especially for instrumentalists. Many music students are eager for any opportunity to play. This can become an outreach of the music department to unchurched musicians.
6. Lists of support ministries. Don't overlook nonmusicians. Publish and distribute lists of support ministries like construction, costume design, electrical, publicity, scenery and poster painting, fund-raising, and other nonmusical needs.

Trying to create an effective, growing music program from scratch is sort of a catch-22. A good music program attracts good musicians, but you need good musicians to have a good music program.

You can chase your tail. You can fold your hands and wait for those good musicians to show up on the church doorstep. Or you can start with whatever and whomever you have.

"If you think you are too small to do a big thing, try doing small things in a big way."

—Author Unknown

When my husband and I left associate positions on a large church staff to pastor a church of our own, I found myself facing this dilemma. The music resources I started with totaled two terrified soloists who hadn't sung since high school glee club, a sound system that was shipped via Noah's ark, an organist who had been playing for all of six months, and on the piano, Yours Truly, who had passed piano proficiency in college eleven years previous and then had promptly forgotten all of it.

The soloists sang with accompaniment tapes. The organist and I practiced a lot, both separately and together, working our way through the keys an accidental at a time. My husband and I created our own little "Microphone of the Month" club by purchasing a new mike or other sound equipment one piece at a time—provided the church mortgage and light bill had been paid that month.

And it got better. (After all, how could it have gotten worse?) Because I provided the opportunity to sing, as new believers joined the church other soloists came forward. Those who were inexperienced or were "unknown quantities"—to me anyway— were allowed to debut on Sunday or Wednesday evenings when visitors were scarcer and it was "just family." I explained to would-be soloists that this is my policy with first-timers, and that there is less pressure with a smaller crowd.

All of them have grown immensely, not only musically but in ministry and in confidence. The organist eventually left us, but we've since gained a drummer, wind and brass players, a couple more keyboard players, and a guitarist, all of whom stepped forward because they saw others being given the opportunity to minister through music.

Expectations and Standards

Ministers who've been around the church block a few times say that individual churches have personalities, much as people do. After you've been in more than one or two, you begin to see the truth of that statement.

Churches have different histories and different leadership; they're made up of different people with their own unique experiences; churches even come into existence for different reasons. Consider the contrasts between a church that was pioneered by an individual when there were no other churches in the area versus a church that was lovingly and carefully birthed by a nearby "mother" church versus a church that was the result of a local church split. The three would exhibit radically different "personality traits."

These personality differences make a minister's life more interesting, to say the least. It makes it nearly impossible to carry a fixed set of expectations to every place of ministry because those expectations are sure to be disappointed in some ways but surpassed in others.

I've learned, particularly in a small church setting, that I can lower my expectations without lowering my standards. We didn't have enough singers to form a choir, so we called it a worship team, and they helped to teach new choruses and lead the congregation in worship.

When we did finally have enough people to start a choir, the first rehearsal completely blew away all my expectations. Mike, one of the newly recruited men, asked in all sincerity, "What do you mean when you say, 'Sing parts'? Do you mean we sing only part of the song?" Neither he, nor several others present, had any frame of reference to understand the concept of harmony.

We began with unison singing. We moved to dividing into men and women in unison, then two-part harmony, and finally four parts. Nine months later we presented our first Christmas musical, and Mike sang the tenor part from memory.

I had to lay aside some expectations. I had previously had choirs with a large percentage of music readers, strong section leaders, and experienced church choristers. The challenge for me as a director had been to keep up the pace and to challenge the choir. Now my challenges were completely different. I had to explain concepts I took for granted and encourage beginning singers to keep trying.

I could not reasonably expect three altos, four sopranos, and two tenors to sound like the fifty-voice choir I heard in my head. I could not expect them to sight-read a piece the first or third or even fifth time.

But lowered expectations do not mean lowered standards. I could and did expect them to watch me, to perform precise entrances and cutoffs, to enunciate their words clearly, and to improve on a piece each time they sang it. I had to discover what their best effort was and then require it of them.

Providing the Right Tools

One of my favorite old TV sitcoms, "The Dick Van Dyke Show," has this great scene when Rob's jeep breaks down in the middle of nowhere. Rob, knowing nothing about automotive repair, pops the hood, looks in, and says, "Yep, there it is—the engine."

Sometimes we ask someone to lead in an area of music ministry, perhaps to direct a children's choir, and they may know nothing about it. They are likely to go to their first rehearsal, open the door and look in at the children bouncing off the walls, and mutter, "Yep, there it is—the kids choir."

It's intimidating to feel so unprepared. As music ministers, we need to equip those we recruit. Here are some tools:

- Internship. Allow a potential director to follow you around, see how you organize and plan for a production, watch you write up a rehearsal schedule, stand by your side as you conduct. Let him learn by watching, little by little learning to do it himself.

- Workshops. If you've ever attended a music convention or workshop and come away enthusiastic and ready to make music, imagine how wonderful it would be to have others working with you who feel the same way. Encourage your directors and potential directors to come to workshops and conventions with you, and do everything in your power and the church's means to make it feasible for them to attend.

- In-house seminars. If it's just impossible for your laypeople to get away for a workshop, have a workshop expert come to them. Call a large church in a nearby area, invite a speaker you met at a convention, prevail upon a music colleague, or even do it yourself.

- Task forces. Unlike a committee, a task force has a specific purpose and a limited existence. Appoint a potential director or leader to a specific project, preferably one that will last three to six months at most. Let her gain some leadership experience without committing her—or you—to a long-term position. If she does well, you can always discuss a more permanent place of leadership.

• Director's notebooks. Get a big three-ring binder for the director of each group or potential group in your music department. Fill it with everything that relates to that group and present it to the director as a tailor-made resource kit. He should be responsible for keeping it up to date so that when leadership of the group changes, the notebook can be passed on to the new director.

What to Put in a Director's Notebook

1. The group's past programs, rehearsal schedules, flyers, recruitment themes, formal rules or requirements
2. Attendance lists, names, addresses, and phone numbers of the members, as well as those of support personnel: sound and lighting technicians assigned to that group, parents (if it's a children's group), assistants, people who have helped in past productions
3. News releases about the group and its past performances
4. Repertoire lists detailing what music the group has performed in the past, what musicals it has performed, what is in the church music library
5. Inventories of props, scenery, costumes, or equipment available to the group, and where items are stored
6. Any pertinent magazine articles or workshop notes that could help the director of the group

---

Motivating People

As ministers of music, one of our biggest challenges and joys is to cultivate and nourish others in ministry and service to the Lord. It isn't easy, but it is worth the effort.

Unfortunately, we sometimes become discouraged by the lack of commitment, the fickleness of human nature, the good intentions that fizzle before they are acted on. In our frustration we may fall into the trap of trying to motivate others to service by making them feel guilty.

Guilt may occasionally motivate people but only for a little while. More often it drives people away. Guilt is what the enemy uses to beat us down and convince us we're not worthy to serve God. Conviction is what the Holy Spirit uses to make us want to repent and serve God. But remember, only God can convict. So lay down those guilt prods, and get creative about motivating others to join you in ministry.

The best motivator I know is the one we started with: communication! If you can share your vision for a music ministry that glorifies God, edifies the believers, and reaches out to the unsaved—and others can latch onto that vision and make it theirs, they'll be your best recruiters.

And if you want to keep your fellow "visionaries" motivated, then your theme song needs to be "Accentuate the Positive, Eliminate the Negative." Focus on what people do well and allow them room and time to grow in their areas of inexperience. A part of your role as talent agent includes cheering on those you've recruited to ministry. Be their biggest fan!

When those inevitable moments of discouragement come

"Recruitment rule #1: Speak softly, and carry a big baton."

along, when you've asked nine parents to act as room monitors during children's choir rehearsal and you've been turned down nine times, remind yourself what Talent Agency you're working for. Keep before you the goal, not that of fame or fortune, but that of helping the members of the body of Christ find their function in it. And remember, you're not getting a measly 10 percent of something that "moth and rust will corrupt" but bountiful royalties of heaven that will last forever.

7

The Producer's Hat

Pulling off a major musical in the church is not unlike producing one of those biblical epics for the wide screen. Or at least it feels that way to the music minister with a thousand pesky details gnawing at her.

- What kind of scenery do we need? More to the point, who'll make it?
- Did anyone rent the spotlight yet? Who's going to pick it up?
- Do we need a fire permit to carry those candles in the processional? Who will apply for the permit? And who'll clean up the wax drippings?

This is the stuff nightmares are made of.

My preproduction nightmares usually start several weeks before Christmas. Although the specifics change, the general plot always goes like this:

The scene opens at the church with the protagonist—me—showing up for the big event. The plot conflict is that I am (a) late, (b) unclothed, or (c) unaware that this is the evening of the musical; hence I have (a) forgotten my music, (b) forgotten my clothes, or (c) all of the above.

My husband has learned to cope with these side effects of my chosen profession. He calmly wakes me up with the semireassuring words, "It's okay, it was just a dream. You have several weeks till the program."

These are not words to go back to sleep on.

Get Help from Others

Lying there in the dark after those nightmares I've learned some things about planning and organizing. The first, most important lesson is to get help. Even Cecil B. De Mille didn't do it alone. You can do anything if you don't mind who gets the credit. If you just said, "Ouch!" you're like many of us in ministry who are working ourselves silly because we don't think anyone else can do it as well as we can, or because we don't want to share the glory.

My biggest headaches in producing a musical are the physical details: scenery, props, costumes. I've learned that, almost without fail, when I have asked others to handle those aspects of a production, they have done far better than I could have done.

And I've frequently been surprised at who will help. Dalene, a children's choir director, hesitated to ask Lee, a grandmother of one of the singers, for help with the scenery. Lee was quite artistic but in recent years suffered from painful arthritis

"The ark scenery is perfect. Now, can you make it rain?"

Dalene approached her hesitantly about assisting with ideas for the scenery; to her surprise, Lee not only offered to design and paint it, she volunteered her husband, Stan, to build it! The two of them created an elaborate rainbow set with a myriad of detailed props like butterflies and flowers, and both Stan and Lee insisted that the painting had been good physical therapy for Lee's arthritis.

Once you've asked for help, it's important to give both freedom and guidance at the same time. Balancing these seemingly conflicting needs is sort of like spinning plates on sticks—you may break a few plates before you get the hang of it.

If you're working with someone who has helped you before, you probably have a good idea of how much freedom you can allow. But if you're not sure, I believe it's better to err on the side of too much, rather than too little, freedom.

Major corporations have done studies on how the individual autonomy and creative freedom of their employees affect a company's success. They've found that giving the employees authority to create new ideas and see them through to completion has dramatically increased the company's ability to keep up with and even anticipate their consumers' needs. In the church realm, creative freedom is not only a means to an end—a "successful" production—but an end in itself, allowing each member of the Body to find his place and function in it.

> *"Today we are replacing the manager as order giver with the manager as teacher, facilitator, and coach. The order giver has all the answers and tells everyone what to do; the facilitator knows how to draw the answers out of those who know them best—the people doing the job."*
>
> —John Naisbitt and Patricia Aburdene, Authors

A word of caution, however: If the person is an unknown quantity to you, it's best to establish deadlines, money limits, and other guidelines up front, preferably in writing.

Let's say you've asked Joan to take care of the table setting for the Living Last Supper pageant. If you don't care what she spends or how it looks, turn her loose. But if you don't want red stemware or a bill for $74.50, give Joan some limits in advance. Write down what her spending limit is and explain that anything beyond it will have to be approved in advance, unless she wants to donate it. That usually inhibits even the most carefree shopper. Provide her with a list of suggested foods and tableware, or better yet, ask her to give you one to approve. And give her a date by which to have it done.

Who to Ask for Help

Where to start when asking for help is always a problem. Consider these sources:

Start with (1) those in the music department who are not already overwhelmed with responsibilities in other departments of the church. Then branch out to (2) parents, spouses, relatives, and friends of those in musical groups.

Look around for those (3) "fringe people" who attend the church but are not actively involved in a ministry. Sometimes all it takes is the camaraderie that comes from participating in a special event to make them feel a part of the church family.

And don't overlook (4) any age-group. One minister of music asked the seniors group to make costumes for a biblical pageant and got far better workmanship than he could have bought—and all at the cost of materials only. Consider youth members for spotlight operators and stagehands. Kids can help publicize their own productions with poster contests and hand-colored program covers.

Finally, prayerfully consider asking for help from (5) unchurched spouses, friends, and coworkers of the folks in your choir. Over and over we've seen men whose construction or technical skills, put to use on a Living Christmas Tree or other production, gave them a sense of accomplishment and belonging that drew them through those church doors.

Start Planning Early

Another way to reduce the frequency and intensity of those late-night dreams of horror before major productions is to get started early.

As incongruous as it seems to listen to Christmas music while the kids are cavorting in the backyard pool, that's when to start. And the directors I know who piece together or write scripts for their own Christmas Tree or Carol Sing programs begin even earlier (like right after New Year's Day).

In my experience, starting early for Christmas hasn't been the biggest challenge. Easter—now there's the tricky date, always changing, sneaking up on you in March when you least expect it! And it's difficult enough to juggle Christmas rehearsals with family celebrations, gift buying, and the round of parties and banquets, let alone find time to listen to Easter music.

One way to combat Early Easter Stress Syndrome is simple—look at your calendar, preferably before February. Find out when Easter is, then work backward to find out how many weeks of preparation time there will be between New Year's Day and Easter. Chances are you'll have to select and order music while eating Thanksgiving turkey leftovers. That way you can begin rehearsals shortly after the Christmas tree is set out on the curb.

Another stress-saver is to make plans for the following year immediately after finishing an Easter musical. If you do an annual Living Last Supper, Living Cross, or Holy Week pageant, make notes afterward, while it's still fresh in your mind, about changes you think would improve it, or music you would like to include, and start a file. If you see or hear a wonderful Easter musical at another church or at a music convention, order a sample copy for yourself and add it to your file. You'll congratulate yourself later, as Christmas bells ring in your ears, that you had the foresight to begin your Easter preparations early.

Whatever you do, don't procrastinate! You're going to need to start early if you plan to memorize the musical.

Living Last Supper Checklist

1. Set the date(s) the program will be presented.
2. Select a script or adapt your own from the biblical accounts.
3. Select and order music that underscores the biblical narrative of the Last Supper and Easter season.
4. Prepare a copy of the script for each participant.
5. Immediately after New Year's, select thirteen men to be involved. Determine who will grow their own beards and who will need synthetic beards.
6. Set rehearsal dates; give a schedule to each disciple, narrator, musician, and sound and lighting technician.
7. Select coordinators for props (table and benches), costumes, makeup, scenery, and food (including tableware).
8. Lay out—or have a publicity coordinator lay out—all posters, flyers, newspaper ads, and news releases for the program. Arrange for a news photographer to take black-and-white photos at least a week before the performance during a rehearsal with full scenery, costumes, and makeup.
9. Meet with the ushers and discuss the offering, Communion (if it will be served), and how to handle latecomers with the least amount of disturbance once the program is underway.
10. Recruit a work crew to help remove and replace the platform furniture or have the props coordinator recruit them.

Have the Choir Memorize the Music

"My choir could never memorize a whole musical!"

"There's barely enough time to learn the music, let alone memorize it!"

"My choir members would quit if I told them they had to perform the whole cantata without books!"

These are just a few of the excuses we make for not requiring our choirs to memorize. I know. I've used them myself.

But Bob showed me differently. When my husband and I arrived on the staff of a large church, Bob, a talented layman who kept the choir going between music ministers, had already paved the way for me.

"I made them memorize the Christmas musical," he told me. "They grumbled, but they did it." He encouraged me not to let them slip back into their previous habit of performing with musical scores.

Since then I've had the opportunity in a small church to build an adult choir from the ground up. They were aghast at the thought of singing their first musical without books. "What'll we hide behind?" could be read in their panic-stricken eyes.

But they did it and did it well. Were they ever proud!

The advantages of memorizing a musical far outweigh any difficulties in learning or preparation. And I'm not convinced that using written music during the performance guarantees more musical accuracy. For one thing, singers without books are much more alert and more responsive to the conductor. They actually look up! They follow more closely because they have to depend on the conductor instead of their books.

Because they look up, they're also more expressive. Without pages in the way of eye contact, the singers are more intent on expressing the words they sing. They just sparkle more! It's not long before they realize they are really ministering.

You can implement some strategies to help your choir memorize their music.

Start with a memorization schedule. I tried this first as an experiment. After finding that the choir members who had had the most trouble memorizing were the ones who came to rely most on the schedule, I adopted the experiment as an effective method of memorization.

To build a memorization schedule I sit down with a calendar and the musical score. I list every rehearsal until the performance, including portions of regular choir rehearsals designated for the musical and extra rehearsals devoted strictly to the musical. I count how many songs the choir has to learn, not counting solos or duets without choral parts. I usually assign two or three songs to each rehearsal by writing the titles next to the rehearsal date.

Two or three rehearsals later (depending on the difficulty of the song and the amount of time I have), I write "Memorized" next to one of the titles. This lets the choir members know the latest date they can use music on this song. On the next rehearsal date, I replace the memorized song with one we haven't rehearsed yet, and so on, until all have been marked "Memorized." Each choir member gets his or her own copy of the schedule at the beginning of the rehearsal season.

Deciding how much time to allot for each song is a combination of studying the music and plain old guesswork. I try to begin with a song that I think will be easy to memorize—it's a good psychological boost for the choir members to check one off early in the rehearsal season.

If I'm short on rehearsals and long on music, I often schedule two "half songs" (where a large portion of the song will be performed by a soloist, but there are also choral parts) to be memorized during the same rehearsal. I also leave rehearsal time close to the performance date in case I've guesstimated wrongly. We can always use that extra time for polishing and review.

An added benefit of this memorization schedule is that it forces you as the director to plan ahead in detail and gives you a list of specific checkpoints to measure your progress.

More and more Christian music companies are making professionally-recorded rehearsal tapes available. Some are purchased individually; others sell one tape for each part (SATB—Soprano, Alto, Tenor, Bass) and give the church permission to make the number of copies they need. When the choir members get their Christmas book in the fall, they get a cassette with their part recorded on it.

If rehearsal tapes are not available commercially, make your own. I've used singers from my choir for tenor, bass, and sometimes first soprano parts and recorded alto and second soprano myself. I write to the publisher explaining what I would like to do and ask for permission. Some ask for a small fee per tape; others charge nothing but ask that the tapes be destroyed after the performance date. I have yet to have a publisher turn me down.

If your church has a nonexistent music budget, consider asking the choir members to purchase their own rehearsal tapes. There's a lot to be said for having them make an investment in the musical.

If professionally recorded rehearsal tapes aren't available and you don't have the singers or the equipment to record your own, a portable tape recorder and a piano playing the voice part is still better than nothing. Most people need to listen to their parts over and over in order to memorize them—tapes let them do that without eating into precious rehearsal time. The tapes also serve to reinforce and review what has already been memorized.

These tools—the memorization schedule and the rehearsal tape—should not be the only ones you own. But think of them as a starter kit and add what works for you and your choir.

Sample Memorization Schedule*

Wed., Aug. 5: "Like a Child"; "Glory to God"

Wed., Aug. 12: "Like a Child"; "Glory to God"

Wed., Aug. 19: "Like a Child" (Memorized); "Glory to God"

Thurs., Aug. 20: "Glory to God" (Memorized); "Light of the World"

Wed., Aug. 26: "Light of the World"; "Go Tell It-Amen"

Wed., Sept. 2: "Light of the World" (Memorized); "Go Tell It-Amen"

Wed., Sept. 9: "Go Tell It-Amen" (Memorized); "He Came to Love Us"

Wed., Sept. 16: "He Came to Love Us"; "Sing Christmas" & "Sing Christmas Reprise"

Thurs., Sept. 17: "He Came to Love Us" (Memorized); "Sing Christmas" & "Reprise"

Wed., Sept. 23: "Sing Christmas" & "Reprise"; "That Name"

Wed., Sept. 30: "Sing Christmas" & "Reprise" (Memorized); "That Name"

Wed., Oct. 7: "That Name"; "Christmas Medley"

Wed., Oct. 14: "That Name" (Memorized); "Christmas Medley"

Thurs., Oct. 15: Review—First Half

Wed., Oct. 21: "Christmas Medley"; "Carol Medley"

Wed., Oct. 28: "Christmas Medley" (Memorized); "Carol Medley"

Wed., Nov. 4: "Carol Medley"

Wed., Nov. 11: "Carol Medley" (Memorized)

Thurs., Nov. 12: Review—Second Half

Wed., Nov., 18: Troubleshooting, polishing any trouble spots

Wed., Nov. 25: No Choir Rehearsal

Wed., Dec. 2 & 9: Review

Thurs., Dec. 10: Dress Rehearsal

Sun., Dec. 13: "Sing Christmas" Performance

*This schedule was used with a small, inexperienced choir. A more accomplished choir could memorize even more quickly.

Take Care of Those Nagging Details

All right, you've asked for and received help. You've started early. You've planned and memorized. What do you do if you still can't get a good night's sleep?

down what it is that's nagging at you. Is it a little detail you keep putting off? Or just a vague anxiety?

The former is easily dealt with: Write it down and the next day take care of it. Don't procrastinate if it means losing sleep.

Anxiety is a little tougher to deal with, but we have the greatest of resources at our disposal—prayer. Paul said, "Do not be anxious about anything, but in everything, by prayer and petition, with thanksgiving, present your requests to God. And the peace of God, which transcends all understanding, will guard your hearts and your minds in Christ Jesus" (Philippians 4:6–7).

Pray about what is bothering you, detailing it for God, and in the process, for yourself. Anxiety is a general feeling of unease that shrinks when we get specific about it with God. So make Him Executive Producer and have a great musical.

Oh, and sweet dreams.

8

The Sound Technician's Hat

We've all heard the cliché, "I don't know much about art, but I know what I like." That sort of describes how I feel about sound reproduction: I don't know much about the technical aspects, but my musician's ear knows what sounds good.

As the music minister, you may have the responsibility for the church's sound system dropped in your lap. You may find yourself overseeing a lot of hardware that you don't understand and wearing the chief technician's hat by default.

If so, don't let the mysteries of digital delays, cardioid patterns, and reverberation decay time scare you. Phantom power is not another of Batman's archenemies and an ohm is not a mantra. The basics of how a sound system operates are not that mysterious after all, and most of the technical stuff you can leave to the experts. In fact, you may find, as I did, that your musician's ear will be even more useful than you thought.

The Basics about Microphones

Let's start with what you may already know, or what your musicianship will help you learn, about microphones. There are different types of microphones, and their capabilities determine where you'll use them. The two main types are dynamic and condenser mikes.

1. Dynamic microphones are high quality, but rugged, and can tolerate temperature extremes, moisture, and mishandling

better than condensers. This makes dynamic mikes ideal for kids' choirs, youth tour choirs, and most hand-held uses where the mike may be dropped, blown into, or otherwise abused. (We had one child take a bite out of one of our colored windscreens—heaven knows what he tried to do to the mike!)

2. Condenser microphones are higher quality and more sensitive but also more fragile and more expensive than dynamic mikes. Condensers are often the best choice for suspending or mounting over choirs, at pulpits, or for quiet instruments.

One reason for this is their uniform response, which means they are able to reproduce high or low tones at the same, or nearly the same, volume levels. If you are using one microphone to pick up both your altos and your sopranos, then you can appreciate the advantages of a microphone with uniform response, also called "flat" response, over one without it.

Another reason for using condenser mikes in this way is that it allows the careful treatment they require. Hanging them over the choir or mounting one on the pulpit cuts down on the amount of handling—and mishandling—of these sensitive mikes. They are not usually recommended for hand-held use because of the likelihood of being dropped or blown into (or bitten).

Condenser mikes require a power supply in addition to that of the amplifier; it is supplied through a battery inside the mike or through an external source on the mike line or built into the mixer. This additional supply is called phantom power. So don't rush out to buy condenser mikes for your choir loft without checking to see what type of power they use, and whether your board has phantom power, or whether it can be added to your system.

While dynamic and condenser microphones are the two main types, you should probably be aware of a third type: contact microphones. This mike is especially suited to instruments like the piano, harp, acoustic guitar, violin, and drums. A contact mike actually attaches directly to the instrument and picks up the vibrations from the instrument's surface. It also reduces feedback and "leakage" of sound from nearby instruments. There is even such a thing as a contact condenser microphone, and I wouldn't be surprised to see contact mikes becoming more widely used in churches as the technology advances and the price comes down.

Understanding Microphone Patterns

As a choral conductor, you need to know the most effective way to use your microphones to maximize the sounds you want heard, while minimizing the sounds you don't want heard, for example, Violet Vibrato in the front row and Max Monotone in the bass section. I call this "creative miking," but only to my sound techs—the choir doesn't need to know that all singers are not miked equally.

To make the best use of your mikes, you need to know their pickup patterns, also known as the "directionality" of the microphone. Since contact microphones operate by picking up vibrations on the surface of an instrument, they have no directionality. The three basic pickup patterns follow:

Omnidirectional—picking up sound equally from all directions. You can imagine the nightmare of feedback from this kind of a pattern.

Bidirectional—picking up sound from two directions at opposite poles from each other with almost no pickup on the other two sides.

Unidirectional—picking up the most sound from straight in front of the mike and rejecting sound from the back. It makes perfect sense that this is the most practical and preferable pickup pattern for church use. The other patterns serve their purposes; for example, an omnidirectional mike might be used for a round-table discussion or perhaps for a speaker's lavaliere mike, but for our purposes, unidirectional solves a lot of problems.

Unidirectional patterns are commonly horseshoe-shaped or "cardioid," which simply means heart-shaped, with the vee of the heart in front of the mike. This means that the greatest volume is directly in front of the mike—from the mike to the point of the vee or the curve of the horseshoe—with the volume dropping off at the sides and almost no sound from behind the mike, known as "rear rejection." This rear rejection cuts down on sources of feedback and on audience noise that would otherwise be amplified.

Knowing this helps you place your singers accordingly. Assume you are miking a small vocal ensemble with either hand-held mikes or mikes on stands. Let's say there are three people to each mike. If you want all the singers to pick up equally, the person directly in line with the mike should be farther away than the two on the sides, so that they are standing in a vee or horseshoe, matching the mike's pickup pattern. However, because we know that all singers do not project the same volume, you might want to put your softest singer directly in line with the mike.

Choirs are somewhat more challenging since there are more people to mike, and they generally stand in straight rows, not vees or horseshoes. Just to complicate matters, the pickup patterns for the mikes can cancel each other out where they cross over.

Therefore, it's critical to know your mike patterns. Know where the pickup pattern is most sensitive, where it drops off on the sides, and where the mike patterns cross each other. And then use that knowledge creatively. Put your better voices where they will pick up best, or if they're too powerful, put them where they will not pick up as strongly. Put your "blenders"— you know who they are, the good voices that stay on their parts but don't stand out—at the most sensitive "hot spots." Put your problem voices in the areas where the patterns cross over or where the pattern drops off at the sides.

It'll probably take some experimentation, but if you're tactful, you can move people around to get the balance you're after. If asked, I often explain that not all voices project the same, and I'm seeking to balance that. It's truthful but not judgmental, since I purposely avoid a discussion of the quality of the voices involved. I had to move one sweet, elderly "Violet Vibrato" because she was almost directly in the vee of the cardioid pattern. She'd been hinting that she wanted to be more front and center, and it turned out that I could find a place less in the pickup pattern that was closer to the center. She was happy; I was happy. It doesn't always turn out so well but when it does, it truly feels like creative miking!

Other Sound System Components

Besides microphones, there are speakers, mixers, and amplifiers to consider. Since many of us find ourselves having to buy or replace components piecemeal, it's important to know what each one does and in what ways they need to be compatible with each other.

I asked several professional sound consultants, "What are the most common mistakes churches make regarding their sound systems?" At the top of nearly everyone's list was buying inadequate or mismatched equipment and trying to patchwork it together. One said he frequently sees churches trying to make home stereo equipment, particularly speakers, work in a sanctuary much larger than the equipment was intended for. Another told of a church that just kept hooking up speakers until they had seven speakers burdening one inadequate amplifier. Still another described the joys of crawling under the platform and up in the attic to find the source of a hum in the sound system. It turned out the speakers had been wired with microphone cable instead of speaker wire.

The moral of these stories is "know thy equipment." You don't have to become a sound consultant yourself, but you should at least learn enough to become an educated consumer. Before you go shopping for a new mixing board or new speakers, you need either to know what is compatible with, or can be adjusted to, your other sound components, or to go armed with enough information so that a sound professional can advise you.

"Assuming a church already has a sound system and wants to upgrade, good quality speakers should be their first investment."

—Dan Taylor, Sound Consultant

Nearly every sound professional I talked to said the component that can have the biggest effect on your system is the speakers. All agreed that poor-quality speakers can make even a great system sound terrible; conversely, good speakers can help a less-than-great system sound better. Like high-quality microphones, good speakers should have a uniform response by reproducing extreme high and low tones with equal clarity.

But before you go out and buy better speakers, you have to know what is compatible with your amplifier. The amplifier is the "engine" or power source that runs everything else. How do you determine what is or isn't compatible?

First, the power output ratings of the amplifier need to match the power requirements of the speakers—all the speakers—connected to it. This means you need to know the wattage ratings, which should be labeled on your amplifiers and speakers, unless they're homemade, and ohm ratings, which may not be labeled. If you're not sure of the ohm ratings, look in the equipment's operator's manual. If your church is like ours was when we came, the amplifier was ancient and no one had the faintest idea where an operator's manual was. (It probably was carved on stone tablets.) In such a case, call the manufacturer or a professional audio dealer and ask.

Second, you have to match the impedance of the speakers with the amplifier. This gets a bit technical, and I'm not sure I understand all the technical stuff—or perhaps I should say, I'm sure I *don't* understand all the technical stuff—but it depends on the wattage and ohm ratings combined and how the speakers are wired, in series or parallel.

Matching impedance is important with mixing consoles as well. The mixer is what the microphone cables plug into so you can adjust volume levels, add effects like reverb, if the mixing board has that capability, and basically mix the sound. Low impedance microphones require low impedance inputs on the mixer, unless you use a line-matching transformer. If you hook a tape deck(s) to the mixer, the input on the mixer must be able to handle that type of signal and impedance. Again, there are line matching transformers that convert tape output to a microphone type of signal.

Low impedance mikes and components are vastly preferable. Low impedance microphones allow you much longer cables, while high impedance mikes can be used only with cords up to eighteen feet, unless there is a line-matching transformer on the cable.

There are consoles that combine amplifiers and mixers, called "powered mixers." Some have a built-in phantom power supply and other things like equalizers and effects. Sound consultants frequently recommend separate amplifiers and mixing boards. Their reasons:

- Powered mixers are not usually stereo.

- When a mixer needs repair, you have to take in only one component, whereas an all-in-one unit means your amplifier is in the shop, too, whether it needs repair or not.

- Separate amplifiers generally put out less ambient noise and more power.

However, let me add my own observations based on purchasing two different powered mixers for different size churches:

- There are some good quality powered mixers (with stereo capability) available that are cheaper than buying two separate components of equal quality.

- Stereo sound is not necessarily desirable in a sanctuary anyway, since congregation members have a habit of sitting scattered throughout the building, rather than centered between the speakers.

- When either your mixer or amplifier is out for repair, you're not likely to be able to use the other component anyway.
- In "live application" (meaning the live music in the church services, as opposed to recording or broadcasting), the ambient noise of our powered mixer has been unnoticeable, even to those sitting right next to it.

In Plain English, Please!

1. Feedback. Amplified sound from a speaker that has reentered a microphone; in other words, "sound the second time around."
2. Resistance. In electrical terms, it's the opposition presented by a circuit to the current passing through it, measured in ohms. For most of us, it's not necessary to understand all the physics of ohms of resistance, just that it relates to measuring impedance requirements of speakers and amplifiers.
3. Resonant Frequency Response. The way sound is reflected in a room. Think of the resonance of a student's half-size violin compared to a full-size concert-quality Stradivarius: their resonance is determined by their size, shape of body, type of wood and strings, and even the glue that holds each together. Churches also vary in resonance due to size, shape, height of ceilings, wood or padded pews, carpet or terrazzo floors.
4. Equalization. This is a way of electronically listening to the room's resonant frequency response and adjusting the sound system to compensate. Equalizers are essentially tone controls dividing sound frequencies into octaves (or even smaller intervals, depending on the equalization system). Using electronic equipment such as a "real time analyzer" and a "calibrated microphone," a sound professional sets the equalizers to accommodate the room's acoustics. (Lack of proper equalization is a common cause of feedback problems.)
5. Impedance. An electrical specification measured in ohms. Microphones are rated as either high or low impedance. What you need to know is that low impedance mikes allow you longer cables and more control over feedback. Speakers and amplifiers also have impedance ratings and must be matched accordingly. Do not mismatch low impedance microphones, speakers, or amplifiers with high impedance components. Low impedance is preferable.
6. Phantom Power. A secondary source of power for condenser mikes (the primary source being the amplifier).
7. Ohm. Like a decibel or a hertz, an ohm is the term for a unit of measurement; in this case, measuring electrical resistance.

When to Get Help

It's probably beginning to dawn on you that you can't just walk into Radio Shack and throw a few things in a sack. You don't have to know how to solder or how to wire a speaker cluster. But you should know enough to ask the right questions and buy the right equipment. And that means doing some homework.

Doing homework has shown us (my husband and me) firsthand how, depending on their purpose, a few expensive components can be more economical than a lot of cheaper ones. We replaced six dynamic mikes over the choir loft with two condenser mikes. Although the cost per mike was more, we spent less overall and got a truer sound and better pickup. And those sturdy dynamic mikes, which were still in good condition, were put to more effective use for our adult ensemble as hand-held mikes. But it took a little research to learn the differences between uses for dynamic and condenser mikes and some comparison shopping to get the best deal. In other words it meant doing homework.

> *"The music minister needs to take a management view [in regard to sound]—how to intelligently buy equipment and how to get the most out of what he has."*
>
> —John Virden, Alpha Sound & Lighting

As the church with microphone cable hooked to the speakers learned, there are times when you need to call in the experts. And by expert, I most emphatically do not mean the salesman at the home stereo store in the mall but an audio equipment professional. A part of your homework is getting on the phone with colleagues and friends and asking for recommendations of sound professionals who understand churches.

Getting professional advice doesn't have to be prohibitively expensive. There are audio suppliers and sound consultants who specialize in helping churches. Many of the church music conferences and workshops around the country offer seminars on the basics of sound reproduction, usually with opportunities for question-and-answer times.

"Most people have learned about sound systems by the seat-of-the-pants method."

—Jim McCandliss, Sound Investment Enterprises

And there are some excellent one- and two-day training workshops available for you and your church sound techs. One of the best-known is Sound Shop, by Sound Investment Enterprises. They offer two levels: Sound Shop I, which provides fundamentals of sound geared to beginners, and Sound Shop II for those who are ready for the more technical specifics of using equalizers and effects. One of the best things you can do for your sound techs—and your church—is to send them to a workshop like one of these that is presented from a nontechnical point of view and focuses on live application, rather than recording or technical theory.

It's a cliché, but a little outlay now for professional advice or training for your sound technicians can save money in the long run, the money your church might spend on wrong or mismatched equipment or, more frustratingly, on quality equipment that is improperly or ineffectively used.

What a Professional Sound Consultant Will Look For

The professional sound consultant should have tools and expertise you don't. Some things he should be able to do for your church:

- If the sanctuary is very large or reverberant, the pro needs to "measure" it electronically. One way he does this is by measuring the reverberation decay time (RT60), which is how long it takes sound to decay sixty decibels.
- The pro needs to determine the ambient noise characteristics of the room—noisy air conditioning units quite common in gyms and multipurpose rooms, nearby airports, busy intersections—that a sound system needs to overcome.
- The pro needs to measure room volume. There is a direct relationship between room reverberation and room volume, which affects the intelligibility of spoken words.
- If a room is unfinished, or being refurbished, the pro needs to know the relative arrangement of the room: where the audience, platform, and speakers will be placed.

- The pro should consider each room and each church individually based on their needs. For instance, the different musical tastes and environmental features of a traditional Presbyterian church with wooden floors, pews, and high ceilings versus a Pentecostal church with carpeting, padded seats, and electric guitars require different approaches.

Those Indispensable Sound Technicians

The person running the soundboard can make or break you. After all those hours of rehearsal, that's hard to swallow. But it's true. Mary can sing the most beautiful, touching lullaby to baby Jesus ever composed on state-of-the-art equipment, but if her mike isn't on, or if it's screeching loudly with ear-splitting feedback, the audience will never hear the lullaby (or anything else for a while).

"The sound man does not exist until a problem with the sound system occurs. Then he becomes the center of attention."

—Glen Davis, Church Sound Technician

My father, a church sound tech for several years, has a pet peeve. He maintains that given a flawless performance, no one will ever even think about the man or woman balancing all those microphones, monitors, and tapes with such competence. But at the first squeal of feedback or the first dead air of a missed cue, all heads swivel to stare at the soundboard.

Dad has a unique way of dealing with this sound-technician-identity-crisis syndrome: At rehearsals he wears a battery-powered hat that features a set of continuously blinking lights on the brim.

"That way," he explains, "they'll notice me even when I don't make mistakes."

The sound techs at my church have a similarly creative solution. For weeks before a major production, they secretly plan what bizarre costumes they'll wear for the performances. One year they showed up at the Living Christmas Tree with surgical scrubs, right down to the gloves and masks—tree surgeons, of course.

But not all sound technicians deal with their frustrations that humorously. There are some concrete ways in which we music ministers can improve our working relationships with our sound crews, and hopefully, their effectiveness in their ministry.

1. It's important for us music ministers not to take our sound techs for granted, as though they're part of the equipment like the equalizers and amplifier and mixing console. We need to recognize the sound crew publicly when everyone else is taking their bows at the end of a production. And it doesn't hurt to send them personal notes of appreciation in between or to leave each a liter of his or her favorite soft drink near the soundboard. They need to know they get noticed when they do things well.

2. I've learned I cannot assume the sound technicians know what I want. (And when I forget, they have my permission to remind me.) In most churches, the choir is up front, and the soundboard is in the rear of the sanctuary or up in the balcony. Naturally, the director's attention is focused on those in front of her, the choir and instrumentalists, and she may forget to include those at work behind her.

In a previous church position, we frequently used accompaniment tapes with the choral anthems. Since we had quite a few reel-to-reel tapes, which were then the accompaniment tape of choice, it meant more work for the sound crew, especially in rehearsals when we might go through a half-dozen or more different reels and cassettes. By persistent pleading, reminding, cajoling, and even scolding, my sound people eventually got me to give them directions first before speaking to the choir. Whether I stopped in the middle of a song to correct a choral problem or went through to the end of the tape, they needed to know, "Do you want to go back to the beginning?" "Are you going to move on to the next number on the rehearsal schedule?" "Do you want to pick up right where you cut off?" By remembering to tell the sound crew first, they could be recuing the tape or readying the next one while I worked with the choir on the musical details.

3. We need to include the sound crew in the rehearsal as equal participants. They are often so physically separated from the singers and instrumentalists, it's no wonder they feel like they're in "outer darkness." I began using a microphone to give instructions during rehearsals, which included the sound crew behind me in what was being said to those in front of me, rather

than assuming they could hear me with my back to them. It has the added benefit of saving wear and tear on my vocal cords during long rehearsals. Another way to include the sound crew is to have them come to the platform at the beginning or the end of rehearsal when the group gathers for prayer or devotional times. Ask one of the sound techs to lead in prayer or bring a devotion. Emphasize their part in the music ministry, too.

4. Work out a system of signals with your sound technician during rehearsals. I often ask, "If I need more tape through the monitor, how would you like me to let you know?" I figure if he makes up the signal, he'll be more likely to watch for it or recognize it when he sees it. Sometimes I'll suggest something. The important thing is to agree so that, on those occasions when you need to use them, your signals will communicate, not confuse.

I've worked with quite a cross section of men and a couple of women on sound crews—some prima donnas, some loners, some team players—and I think I know a good sound technician when I see one. These are the qualities I value most:

1. A "Can Do" Attitude. When we rented the local auditorium and presented our first Living Christmas Tree, it was a leap of faith for all of us. As we put the structure together, one of the volunteers frantically buzzed around me all day, saying, "This is never going to work!" "Did you hear about the problem with the lights? We'll never be able to fix it." "We're never going to get this up in time!"

I'm the stoic type, so I kept up a calm exterior, but my stomach was churning. I was scared to death, and I wanted to throttle this guy for feeding my fears. One of the things that kept me sane was my sound guys. Here they were calmly setting up our sound system in a building several times the size of our church. They must have been nervous about running sound in a building we'd never been in before, using a structure and miking we'd never rehearsed with, but thank goodness they didn't feel the need to share that with me. We had some horrendous feedback problems during the dress rehearsal, but they told me, "No problem. We'll stay till we figure it out." And they did, by missing dinner and working to adjust the system until they got rid of the feedback. Since then I've nicknamed them "No Problem" and "You Got It," because those are the attitudes they embody.

"The sound system will work flawlessly until the final rehearsal before a major production. Then it will produce feedback from nowhere."

—Walters' Law of Feedback

2. Quiet cooperation. During rehearsals, particularly those tense, final rehearsals before a production, I tend to become hyperfocused on what needs to be accomplished during the remaining time. The clock is ticking away, my adrenaline is pumping, the construction worker in the bass section is yawning because he has to get up at four-thirty in the morning, and the student in the alto section is looking at her watch because finals are coming up. I feel responsible for how I'm spending their time, and I'm not going to be very open then to what I consider extraneous details. If my sound techs have a problem, suggestion, or comment that can wait till later, it will be much better received then, even if they wait only until the end of the rehearsal and the choir is dismissed. I've worked with sound people who weren't sensitive to what was a pressing matter and what could wait till later, and it was quite frustrating.

A technical rehearsal goes a long way toward eliminating that kind of frustration. For major productions, it's becoming a necessity to have a rehearsal before the dress rehearsal with the light and sound crews, plus any drama, multimedia, or other special effects personnel. That's their time to ask questions, solve technical problems, or make suggestions.

An effective relationship between the music minister and the sound technician is one where each trusts the other. You can pretty well divide church sound reproduction into two parts: what the choir, instrumentalists, and conductor need to hear on the platform, and what the congregation needs to hear in the sanctuary. The sound tech needs to trust the music minister enough to give him what he needs through the monitors and platform sound system; the music minister must trust the sound tech to balance the sound for the congregation. Both need to work together to understand the building's eccentricities and hot spots, and to discover how to get the best sound for each area, platform and sanctuary.

Take that mutual trust, add a generous dose of training, plus a sense of humor, and you've got a mix for an effective sound ministry. You still may not understand much about the physics of sound, but you'll like what you hear.

Tips from the Techs

- If you use condenser microphones with batteries, assume they'll go out at the worst possible moment and always have spares. (This goes for bulbs, fuses, cables, and anything else that could foul up a production.)
- Keep a notebook with specs on each piece of sound equipment the church owns: wattage, ohm ratings, etc. (It wouldn't hurt to keep operator's manuals in there, too.)
- The best location for the soundboard is where the true sound of the building is (usually two-thirds from the front in the center)—not in an enclosed booth.
- When building or refurbishing the platform, always install twice as many microphone outlets as you think you'll ever need.
- When buying a mixing board, always get one with more channels than you think you'll ever need.
- Trust your ear more than you trust your sliders, faders, and meters. If something doesn't sound right, but your equipment tells you it should, keep searching until you find the problem.

9

The Musician's Hat

Dear Musician Friend,
  You sounded pretty down on yourself in your last letter. You seem pretty sure that, because you're not a highly trained musician, you're going to be a failure as a music minister.

Not necessarily.

Sure, musical training is important! You've definitely got your work cut out for you. But remember, the musician's hat is only one of many that you'll be wearing. You feel God has called you to this ministry; you love the people and the pastor; I know you're patient and a hard worker—next to all those things, sharpening your musical skills is easy!

I'm no Ph.D. on the subject but maybe I can give you a few basics to get you started.

Be Prepared

First, when it comes to rehearsals, there is no substitute for preparation. Prepare, prepare, prepare! And if you're feeling insecure, prepare some more! Toscanini once said, "The rehearsal is the conductor's performance." If you've attempted even one rehearsal, I'm sure you've discovered the truth of that statement.

Plan everything in detail: which music you'll rehearse, what order you'll do it in, how much time you'll spend on each piece, where you want the singers to sit, and even when you want them to stand during rehearsal.

"Okay, choir, be sure to count through the rests."

Learn How to Conduct

After you've planned all that, practice conducting each piece. By the way, do you know the basic conducting patterns? Here's a basic starter kit:

2 beats per measure: ($\frac{2}{2}$, $\frac{2}{4}$, fast $\frac{6}{8}$)
3 beats per measure: ($\frac{3}{4}$, fast $\frac{9}{8}$)
4 beats per measure: ($\frac{4}{4}$, $\frac{12}{8}$)
6 beats per measure: (slow $\frac{6}{8}$)

Of course, there are other combinations of 2 and 3, like $\frac{5}{4}$, but I don't consider those basic. There are even variations on the ones I've listed, but I've found these to be the simplest and clearest, with definite downbeats and unequivocal upbeats that come from the outside in.

Practice tracing these patterns in the air. If you're left-handed, you will still have to beat time with your right hand—it's too confusing for accompanists and singers if you don't!

In fact, until you get comfortable with these patterns, just forget about your left hand. (Or if it keeps wanting to cut in, tie it behind your back.)

"It is not the job of the left hand to mimic the right."

—Stephen W. Plate, Music Professor

Now it's time for some serious reflection. Put on a tape and practice conducting to the mirror. Forget all those cartoons you've seen with the conductor thrashing wildly about, slicing and dicing a six-foot section of air. Keep the beat centered in front of your upper body with a precise point for each beat (called the "ictus") and a very slight rebound, or bounce, after each ictus.

Once you've got these basic patterns down, you've learned to walk. But you'll want to run, float, march, dance, stomp, tiptoe, and skip, too. Keep going back to that mirror to experiment and refine the many moods you can convey through the same patterns.

Learn Cues and Body Language

Okay, now you can untie that left hand. Your left hand's job is to cue entrances and cutoffs for instrumental or vocal sections,

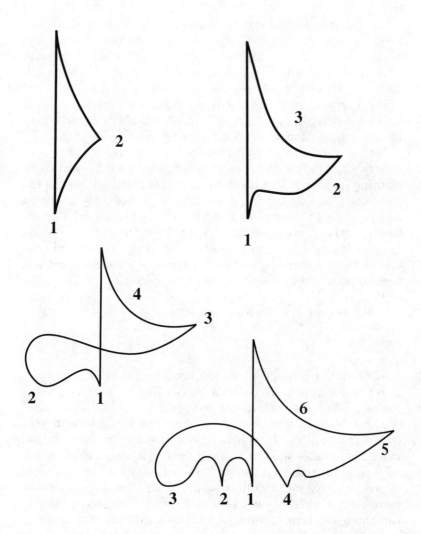

to add emphasis at the beginning of a piece or at a change of meter or tempo, and to fine-tune the piece with gestures controlling the volume level (or anything else you can make it work for).

For example, I often use my left hand to signal my choir that we're approaching the second ending, or coda (two fingers up), to tell them to enunciate (forefinger pointing to my chin) or to remind them of a unison section (one finger up). I always tell them not to worry unless they see me holding my nose!

You'll have to experiment with what signals work for you and your groups, but generally, palms raised indicates you want more volume; palms down or palms facing the group shushes them.

Just be sure that whatever you're doing is clear to everyone. Otherwise, it only signals confusion. I once made the mistake of pointing up at the microphones hanging over the loft just as the choir stood to sing the Sunday morning anthem. My intention was to remind the men, who had the first entrance in that particular anthem, to project up and out. Unfortunately, the sound guys, thinking I was cuing them, started the accompaniment tape before I was ready, and the entrance was a mess! (And yes, I *had* practiced that piece in front of the mirror!)

> *"The conductor is . . . the traffic cop, making sure everyone is playing at the same speed and the same volume."*
>
> —André Previn, Conductor

After all this talk about beating time, I want to caution you— Don't feel trapped or confined by conducting patterns. Once you're comfortable with them, take some risks: Use your hands (both of them) in more expressive ways, particularly with your choral groups. I've noticed that instrumentalists generally feel more comfortable with unadorned beat patterns, but when you add singers, the lyrics open up a whole new dimension of expression. As someone has said, "You're the conductor—be more than a metronome, be *musical*." Use your face, your posture, and your body to convey what you want from your choir.

A university chorale director I had would let his arms hang limp at times and conduct with his body. We took our entrance and cutoff cues from watching him breathe. It taught me a lot about the value of body language and breathing with a choir.

So go back to the mirror and breathe the song. Pretty soon you'll be able to direct with both hands tied behind your back.

Oh, and one last word about body language. While you're at the mirror, check your facial expression, because your choir is going to reflect what they see in you. One conductor was so intense he grimaced at the choir. They sounded great but they looked as though they were in pain!

"Conducting is a real sport. You can never guarantee what the results are going to be so there's always an element of chance. That's what keeps it exciting."

—Aaron Copland, Conductor and Composer

Select Music Wisely

Another tough musical chore is selecting music and, like conducting, one you'll get better at with experience.

One thing I've learned by doing is to spot the potential stumbling blocks in a piece of music. But they're not the same for every group and I still get surprised. For example, it still catches me off guard how many singers find it hard to learn a "background" part (one where the choir is sustaining an "ooh" or "ah" behind a soloist). My theory is that it's because most people don't count well, or perhaps the soloist on melody throws them off. But I'm learning not to assume that those "background" vocals will take only a few minutes of rehearsal time.

Other common trouble spots are also rhythm-related: triplets, dotted eighths, syncopated beats, unexpected rests. Look through the music for these and make sure you know how to sing them correctly before you attempt to teach them to your choir. Check to see if a musical phrase or chorus is repeated with different rhythms or harmonies, so you can forewarn your singers.

There's another simple tip-off to musical trouble spots. If you're at a music conference sight-reading through new music, circle the sections everyone stumbles over. I always figure if a roomful of music ministers are having trouble with a piece, it's a sure bet their choirs will have the same difficulty.

When you're choosing music, don't automatically discard it if it has trouble spots in it. Just weigh the cost (how much rehearsal time it will require) against the finished product (the effect you hope to achieve) and decide if it's worth the expenditure of time and effort.

It probably goes without saying, but I'll say it anyway: You want to strive for variety and balance in selecting music. But it's tough to do. For one thing, I know what I like, and it's hard to pick something I don't like. I also know what my choir and congregation like (usually) and I don't want to buck them. (Have you ever tried to teach an adult choir a song they don't like? They're worse than kids!)

The only remedy I know of is exposure. Expose yourself to all kinds of musical styles—not just your favorites (and not just church music, either). Ask musical friends what they're listening to these days. Go to music conferences and concerts with an attitude of learning and growing. Expose your choir and congregation to different groups and artists, perhaps through a concert series, again challenging them to learn and grow.

Last and *most* important, select music based on the message. Are the lyrics biblically sound? Do they express something important? Is there a balance between those songs that are testimonies ("I"- and "me"-related) and worship songs (focused on God or addressing Him directly)? Does the music express the lyrics in a compatible way?

Several years back a song came out with the lyrics, "I am so happy, so very happy." However, the slow, melancholy music was saying something else entirely! Another case of words and music unequally yoked together is the song "We're Marching to Zion." The $\frac{3}{4}$ signature has prompted more than one musician to suggest that it should be titled "We're Waltzing to Zion." Sometimes a good message can overcome a less than ideal musical setting; nevertheless, bear it in mind when making your choices.

Teach Vocal Techniques Creatively

One of your most difficult tasks is that of teaching abstracts like vocal techniques. In the limited amount of time available in rehearsals, the only way to teach vocal techniques is to give your singers a mental image, a "handle" they can grasp.

For example, how do you explain the concept of tone placement? If you begin with complicated explanations of "soft palates" and "nasopharynxes," you'll have glazed eyes staring back at you. Draw a picture for your singers: "You've just bitten off a mouthful of hot pizza. What do you do?" They'll automatically raise the back of the soft palate, letting air rush in to cool the blistered roof of their mouth. "Okay, that's how much space you want inside your mouth when you sing." Step one to correct tone placement: an open throat.

Other methods include the "semiyawn" approach, where you instruct the singers to try the beginning of a yawn. Again, they should feel the air rush in to the "cool spot" as they lift the soft palate. Make sure they find the difference between the open throat and relaxed tongue of a semiyawn and the stretched throat and pulled-back tongue of a full yawn. My only problem with this approach to teaching an open, relaxed tone is that it makes everyone yawn. I'll bet you're yawning right now! Then, have the singers take a breath, raising the soft palate until they feel the "cool spot," and sing an "ah" vowel without changing the position of their mouth and throat.

To further lift the placement of the tone, have the singers produce the most nasal "ah" they can muster. Then, without changing the nasality, ask them to add the open throat using either the "semiyawn" or "hot pizza" approach.

Imitation and contrast are helpful techniques when you're trying to get across abstract concepts in a limited time. However, I think they should be used very sparingly in private voice lessons, where an overzealous student might damage something trying to emulate his teacher's sound without understanding the fundamentals of voice production.

Merlin Mitchell, minister of music at Central Assembly of God, Springfield, Missouri, recommends imitation and contrast when trying to blend vibratos within a choral section. He may ask the whole soprano section to produce "the wildest, wobbliest tremolo possible," and then a straight tone, and finally, he will ask them to just let a natural, flowing vibrato "be there." He adds, "I never single out an individual and embarrass him/her in front of the group. On a couple of occasions, the singers with faulty vibrato have come to me on their own for further help. It would be a shame to ask a person to leave a choir just because we didn't know how to deal with his/her faulty production."

C. Harry Causey, well-known for his writing and speaking in the field of worship and music, also recommends contrast as a device to teach open, uniform vowel sounds to the choir. Getting singers to produce an "ooh" vowel that isn't tight and pinched is difficult. He says, "Put an 'oh' inside the mouth, purse the lips, then sing, 'moo.' To really get this concept, have the singers do it wrong. Place an 'ee' inside the mouth, purse the lips, and sing the ridiculous sounding 'eeeooo' that results. Now go back to having an 'oh' inside. Sometimes the best teaching is by contrast."

Causey also offers his choir some interesting mental images for "coloring" an "ee" vowel, making it less bright. After instructing them to put more "oo" in the "ee," he might describe it as putting some "blue" in the vowel. Or he might ask the choir to turn up the bass and down the treble. You might come up with some images of your own—the point is to give your singers a concrete handle on an abstract concept.

Breath support is probably the most important vocal concept you want to communicate and, I think, one of the most difficult. By the time singers get into the adult choir, they've heard all kinds of things in junior high glee club. One of them, "Use your diaphragm," they've no doubt heard dozens of times, each time probably wondering, *What in the world is it? Where is my diaphragm anyway? And how do I use it when I'm not sure I can feel it working?*

Rather than discuss the diaphragm, I prefer to focus on the abdominal muscles and rib cage. People who have no idea what or where the diaphragm is know how to suck in their stomach muscles and can feel their rib cages expand. Granted, you and I know the diaphragm is involved in the process, but I don't think it's the mechanism they need to worry about.

Rebecca Smelser calls her "'Horizontal Balloon Method' the 'picture book' path to an often-discussed but rarely understood concept known to singers as 'diaphragmatic breathing.'" She suggests having choir members stand with their hands on either side of their rib cages so they can feel the ribs expand as though a balloon is filling horizontally. (A "vertical" breath is one in which the shoulders and chest move up.) It's easier for the singers to focus on horizontally breathing when they inhale slowly and quietly. Then have them hiss on an "sssss" and empty the lungs slowly and evenly, tucking in body panels from all directions to provide support for the tone. (I would add that the singers should keep the rib cage expanded throughout this exercise.)

She then suggests the following procedure:

- Breathe evenly and slowly on the conductor's preparatory beat.
- Then hold and release on the conductor's cue.
- Repeat this exercise many times at different tempos using the collecting breath on the preparatory breath as an indication of the tempo forthcoming.

The "Horizontal Balloon" is one mental picture. Another is a bellows, which also conjures up the image of something that inflates from side to side but is not as common a picture as a balloon. Put that creative gift of yours to work and come up with effective mental pictures that work for your groups. Perhaps your singers themselves will come up with images or exercises that help communicate abstract vocal concepts. You never know till you try! Remember, you learn by doing.

Develop Skills in Instrumental Arranging

Yet another musical skill that I am learning by doing is arranging for instruments. I was a voice major in college, and now I'm wishing I'd listened more closely in those Orchestration and Form and Analysis classes!

I'm in no position to tell you how to write instrumental arrangements. But I'll tell you how I'm learning (besides digging out all my old college notes). I listen critically to all the praise tapes, accompaniment tapes, and other orchestral and instrumental recordings I can. If I really like something, I try to analyze how the sound was achieved: what instruments are playing, what combination is used. I talk to friends who are far more accomplished at arranging than I am and ask for hints. I attend instrumental seminars at music conferences, even though some are way over my head. I look for articles in church music magazines. I ask my instrumentalists about the ranges and capabilities of their instruments, admitting I am no expert. They're happy to tell me what makes their instruments sound best. And since they're specialists on their instruments, they are sometimes more helpful than the professional arrangers who know a great deal about orchestration as a whole, but may be less familiar with specific instruments.

Be Good to the Church Instruments

Besides arranging for instruments, you'll have to learn something about maintenance, at least for those instruments owned by the church. Once again, the best way to learn is to consult the experts, the people who teach, sell, or play the instrument.

If the church piano service contract has long since expired, who will you get to tune it?

I faced this problem at one church, where it seemed the senior pastor and I could not find a piano tuner who satisfied either of us. One guy would get the piano in tune, but it wouldn't last more than a few weeks; another would leave it little better than he found it; still another would miss appointment after appointment. (Fortunately, my pastor knew quite a bit about piano tuning, and we were in total agreement about the situation.)

I called all the people we could think of who would know about piano maintenance—piano teachers and salespeople, music ministers at other churches in town, music faculty at the local college, even the symphony orchestra—to ask for recommendations. Eventually we found a tuner who showed up on time, tuned the instrument well, and whose work lasted at least six months. Believe me, we put his name and number on every Rolodex card file in the church office!

When you have someone tune the piano, service the organ, or do anything to any of the church's instruments, ask lots of questions. Learn all you can about what they're doing and why—not so that you can check up on them, but so you'll know that much more about taking good care of the instrument.

Is the piano going out of tune every couple of months? Ask the tuner if the room temperature is getting too cold at night, or if the piano needs a dehumidifier, or if it was moved improperly for that children's choir production. Our platform is quite small, making it necessary to move the piano every time we have a special production. At the advice of a piano tuner we trust, we've decided to invest in a piano dolly to ease some of the stress on the legs.

Ask questions like: "What can we do to protect this instrument?" "How should it be stored (or covered)?" "Are there temperature requirements we should be aware of?"

In case of repairs: "Is this a normal repair considering the age of this instrument?" "If not, what caused it to need repair?" "What can we do to preserve it or to prevent it from happening again?"

If you're told an instrument needs extensive repair or even replacement, always get more than one opinion. Dealing with all those piano tuners, I learned that every one of them had his own little idiosyncrasies. One would say, "You need to replace these hammers," and another would say, "They're fine." Just like with any major purchase or repair, it pays to shop around.

So learn all you can, and consider everything you learn preventive medicine that can save repair or replacement costs later.

"Shall I tell you the secret of a true scholar? It is this: Every man I meet is my master in some point, and in that I learn from him."

—Ralph Waldo Emerson

In fact, let me encourage you: The most important thing you can do to excel in your role as a musician, or in any of your roles, is to keep learning. Learn through college classes or private tutoring, if you can. Learn from those around you— musicians in your choir or congregation, colleagues in music ministry, workshop speakers at music conferences. Learn from exposing yourself to music, plus read books and articles on music. Learn by trial and error, by taking some calculated risks. I'm learning that it's okay to admit that I don't know everything about every hat on my music ministry hat rack; I'm also finding that other music ministers are eager to share with me what they've learned, if I'll only ask.

And finally, I come back to your call. If you know God has called you to music ministry, you can trust that He'll equip you for the job (with your cooperation, of course). Don't base your worthiness, or lack thereof, on a wall full of degrees or on "musical genes," as wonderful as those things are. You are worthy because of who you are in Christ, and because He has called you to His ministry.

So grab your hats, confirm your call, and hang on! As the Steven Curtis Chapman song says, "This is the great adventure!"

Your friend and fellow student,

Chéri Walters

Endnotes

PAGE

16   "According to Johansson. . . ." Calvin Johansson, "The Professional Director and Volunteer Musicians," *Advance* (April 1982): 29.

17   "(The) pastoral duty. . . ." Calvin Johansson, *Music and Ministry: A Biblical Counterpoint* (Peabody, Mass.: Hendrickson Publishers, Inc., 1984), 33.

32   "Just as no sane pastor. . . ." Lloyd Ogilvie, "What Pastors Wish Choir Directors Knew," *The Choir Director's Handbook*, ed. Andrea Miller Wells (Waco, Tex.: Word, Inc., 1981), 80–81.

38–39   "The extraordinary, lovely thing. . . ." Quoted by Garth Bolinder, *What Every Pastor Needs to Know about Music, Youth, and Education* (Carol Stream, Ill.: Christianity Today, Inc., 1986).

39   "He's not going. . . ." Bill Gaither, Serendipity Music Conference, Los Angeles, Calif., January 1977.

42   "Regardless of the outcome. . . ." Eric Berne, *Games People Play* (New York: Ballantine Books, 1964), 124.

48   "Humor can be used. . . ." William Ellis, *Reader's Digest,* May 1973.

48–49   "As laughter subsides. . . ." Nancy Hoch and Dean Hoch, "Take Time to Laugh," *Reader's Digest*, February 1988, 59.

49   "When once accused. . . ." Dotsey Welliver, *Laughing Together: The Value of Humor in Family Life* (Elgin, Ill.: Brethren Press, 1986), 105.

50   "Once you can laugh. . . ." Susan Seliger, *Stop Killing Yourself: Make Stress Work for You* (New York: G. P. Putnam's Sons, 1984), 195.

PAGE

54 "Don't lead—worship." Don Moen, "Worship," PAGE MusiCalifornia, San Diego, Calif., 1990.

57 "John Plastow. . . ." John Plastow, "Contagious Enthusiasm: How to Motivate Your People to Excellence," MusiCalifornia, San Diego, Calif., 1990.

60 "They are real people. . . ." Dan Crace, "Motivation—Your Secret to Success," *The Staff* 4, no. 2 (1982).

63 "It also shows. . . ." Barbara Hemphill, *Taming the Paper Tiger* (New York: Dodd, Mead & Co., 1988), 49.

68–69 "The 'art of wastebasketry. . . .'" Hemphill, *Taming the Paper Tiger*, 32.

119–120 "It would be a shame. . . ." Merlin Mitchell, "The Uncontrolled Vibrato," *The Staff* 3, no. 3 (1982).

120 "Sometimes the best teaching. . . ." C. Harry Causey, "More Exercises for Phonation," *Music Revelation* (April 1990): 2.

120–121 "Rebecca Smelser calls her. . . ." Rebecca Smelser, "Simply Good Singing," *Creator* (November/December 1985): 5.

Resources for the Music Minister

AUDIO AND VIDEO RESOURCES

Church Music Workshop. Magazine, music folio, and audiocassette. United Methodist Publishing House. Cokesbury Subscription Services, P.O. Box 801, Nashville, Tenn. 37202-0801, (800) 672-1789.

Church Office Tax Resource Tapes. Audiocassettes by Richard R. Hammar, J.D., LL.M., CPA. Christian Ministry Resources, P.O. Box 2301, Matthews, N.C. 28106, (800) 222-1840.

A Church Organist's Primer. Instructional videos, volumes 1–2. Sally Cherrington, instructor. Allen Organ Company, 150 Locust Street, P.O. Box 36, Macungie, Pa. 18062-0036, (215) 966-2202.

Clergy Tax Tapes. Audiocassettes by Richard Hammar, J.D., LL.M., CPA. Christian Ministry Resources, P.O. Box 2301, Matthews, N.C. 28106, (800) 222-1840.

Contemporary Keyboard Styles. Instructional videos, volumes 1–4. Kent Henry, Jeff Hamlin, and Tom Brooks, instructors. Psalmist Resources, 9820 East Watson Road, St. Louis, Mo. 63126-9977, (314) 842-6161 or (800) 343-9933.

Family Worship at Christmas. Devotional audiocassette and booklet designed for the four Sundays before Christmas and Christmas Eve by C. Harry Causey. Music Revelation, 7 Elmwood Court, Rockville, Md. 20850, (301) 424-2956.

Gospel Music and Hymns By Ear. Instructional books and audiocassettes. Davidsons, 6727 PR Metcalf, Shawnee Mission, Kans. 66204, (913) 262-4982.

Group Vocal Techniques. Instructional videocassette companion to book of the same name—see section on books. Hinshaw Music, P.O. Box 470, Chapel Hill, N.C. 27514, (919) 933-1691.

Guitar Praise: Improving Your Ability. Instructional videos, volumes 1–4. Kent Henry and Randy Rothwell, instructors. Psalmist Resources, 9820 East Watson Road, St. Louis, Mo. 63126-9977, (314) 842-6161.

How Does God Reveal Himself Through Music. Audiocassette by C. Harry Causey. Music Revelation, 7 Elmwood Court, Rockville, Md. 20850, (301) 424-2956.

How to Improve Your Congregational Singing. Audiocassette by C. Harry Causey. Music Revelation, 7 Elmwood Court, Rockville, Md. 20850, (301) 424-2956.

How to Increase the Size of Your Choir. Audiocassette by C. Harry Causey. Music Revelation, 7 Elmwood Court, Rockville, Md. 20850, (301) 424-2956.

How to Make Your Choir Sound Like a Million. Audiocassette by C. Harry Causey. Music Revelation, 7 Elmwood Court, Rockville, Md. 20850, (301) 424-2956.

How to Take Your Choir on Tour—Happily. Audiocassette by C. Harry Causey. Music Revelation, 7 Elmwood Court, Rockville, Md. 20850, (301) 424-2956.

How to Thaw a Frozen Congregation. Audiocassette by C. Harry Causey. Music Revelation, 7 Elmwood Court, Rockville, Md. 20850, (301) 424-2956.

John Plastow's Choreography That Works! Videocassette. John Plastow, instructor. Plastow Publications/The Drama Store, 1442 E. Lincoln Avenue, Suite 332, Orange, Calif. 92665, (714) 282-2296.

Music Is for Children. Audiocassette and curriculum by Connie Fortunato. David C. Cook Publishers, 850 N. Grove Ave., Elgin, Ill. 60120, (708) 741-2400 or (800) 323-7543.

Music Minister Training Guide. Videocassette series. Volume 1: *Worship Leader Training Guide.* Volume 2: *Choral Leader Training Guide.* Billy Jack Green, Roger Christian, Rick Forbus, and Rick Dinoff, instructors. Church Bionics, P.O. Box 42, Woodstock, Ga. 30188, (800) 635-9087.

New Minister's Guide to Legal and Tax Issues. Audiocassette by Richard R. Hammar, J.D., LL.M., CPA. Christian Ministry Resources, P.O. Box 2301, Matthews, N.C. 28106, (800) 222-1840.

101 Things to Say to Your Choir to Improve Their Sound 100%. Videocassette. Douglas Lawrence, instructor. Thomas House Publications, distributed by Intrada Music Group, Anderson, Ind., (317) 640-8211.

Perfect Pitch Supercourse. Audiocassette and handbook. David L. Burge, instructor. American Educational Music, Inc., Music

Resources Bldg., Dept. CH4, 1106 E. Burlington, Fairfield, Iowa 52556, (515) 472-3100.

Rhythm, Rhyme, and Rehearsals—The Kathie Hill Children's Workshop. Videocassette. Kathie Hill, instructor. StarSong Communications, 2325 Crestmoor, Nashville, Tenn. 37215, (800) 835-7644.

Staff Training Tape — Copyright Law: Questions and Answers. Audiocassette available as a "Church Copyright Law Kit" along with reference book *The Church Guide to Copyright Law* and fifty four-page brochures, "Copyright Law—Brochures for Church Workers," by Richard R. Hammar, J.D., LL.M., CPA. Christian Ministry Resources, P.O. Box 2301, Matthews, N.C. 28106, (800) 222-1840.

Theatre Production in the Local Church. Audiocassettes. John Plastow, instructor. Plastow Publications/The Drama Store, 1442 E. Lincoln Avenue, Suite 332, Orange, Calif. 92665, (714) 282-2296.

The Vocal Coach Speakers Video Workshop. Videocassette. Chris and Carole Beatty, instructors. StarSong Communications, 2325 Crestmoor, Nashville, Tenn. 37215, (800) 835-7644.

What is Worship? Audiocassette by C. Harry Causey. Music Revelation, 7 Elmwood Court, Rockville, Md. 20850, (301) 424-2956.

Books

Children and Youth

Choksy, Lois. *The Kodaly Method.* Englewood Cliffs, N.J.: Prentice-Hall, Inc., 1988.

Fortunato, Connie. *Children's Music Ministry: A Guide to Philosophy and Practice.* Elgin, Ill.: David C. Cook, 1982.

Jacobs, Ruth K. *The Successful Children's Choir.* Tarzana, Calif.: H. T. Fitzsimmons, 1948.

Layton, Dian. *Soldiers with Little Feet.* [Children's praise and worship] Shippensburg, Pa.: Destiny Image Publishers, 1989, (800) 722-6774.

Nye, Robert Evans, and Vernice Trousdale Nye. *Music in the Elementary School.* Englewood Cliffs, N.J.: Prentice-Hall, 1964.

Osbeck, Kenneth W. *My Music Workbook.* [For junior choirs] Grand Rapids, Mich.: Kregel Publications, 1982.

Church Music Ministry

Are, Thomas L. *Please Don't Ask Me to Sing in the Choir.* Carol Stream, Ill.: Hope Publishing Co., 1985.

Bock, Fred and Lois. *Creating Four-Part Harmony.* Carol Stream, Ill.: Hope Publishing Co., 1989.

Bolinder, Garth. [Music section] *What Every Pastor Needs to Know about Music, Youth, and Education.* Carol Stream, Ill.: Christianity Today, Inc., 1986.

Causey, C. Harry. *Things They Didn't Tell Me about Being a Minister of Music.* Rockville, Md.: Music Revelation, 1988.

Ferguson, John A., and Joy E. Lawrence. *A Musician's Guide to Church Music.* New York: The Pilgrim Press, 1981. $\mathcal{M} \; T \; 8 \; 8 \; L \; 39$

Hooper, William L. *Ministry and Musicians.* Nashville, Tenn.: Convention Press, 1986.

Hustad, Donald P. *Jubilate! Church Music in the Evangelical Tradition.* Carol Stream, Ill.: Hope Publishing Co., 1981.

Johansson, Calvin M. *Music and Ministry: A Biblical Counterpoint.* Peabody, Mass.: Hendrickson Publishers, Inc., 1984. $\mathcal{M} \; L \; 3 \; 869.563$

Mapson, J. Wendell, Jr. *The Ministry of Music in the Black Church.* Valley Forge, Pa.: Judson Press, 1984.

Mitchell, Robert. *Music and Ministry.* Philadelphia, Pa.: Westminster Press, 1978.

Osbeck, Kenneth W. *The Ministry of Music.* Grand Rapids, Mich.: Kregel Publications, 1975. *ordered?*

Routley, Erik. *Church Music and the Christian Faith.* Carol Stream, Ill.: Agape, 1978.

_____. *Music Leadership in the Church.* Nashville, Tenn.: Abingdon Press, 1967.

Topp, Dale. *Music in the Christian Community.* Grand Rapids, Mich.: William B. Eerdmans Publishing Co., 1976.

Wohlgemuth, Paul W. *Rethinking Church Music.* Carol Stream, Ill.: Hope Publishing Co., 1981.

Devotionals

Lucado, Max. *The Applause of Heaven.* Waco, Tex.: Word Publishers, 1990.

Osbeck, Kenneth W. *Devotional Warm-ups for the Church Choir.* Grand Rapids, Mich.: Kregel Publications, 1985.

Hymnody

Bailey, Albert Edward. *The Gospel in Hymns.* New York: Charles Scribner's Sons, 1950.

Bock, Fred, and Bryan Jeffery Leech, eds. *The Hymnal Companion.* Nashville, Tenn.: Paragon Associates, Inc., 1979.

Dudley-Smith, Timothy. *Lift Every Heart.* Carol Stream, Ill.: Hope Publishing Co., 1984.

Eskew, Harry, and Hugh T. McElrath. *Sing with Understanding: An Introduction to Christian Hymnody.* Nashville, Tenn.: Broadman Press, 1980.

Hustad, Donald P. *Dictionary-Handbook for Hymns for the Living Church.* Carol Stream, Ill.: Hope Publishing Co., 1978.

Lovelace, Austin. *The Anatomy of Hymnody.* Chicago, Ill.: G.I.A. Publications, Inc., 1982.

_____. *The Organist and Hymn Playing.* Carol Stream, Ill.: Agape, 1981.

Osbeck, Kenneth W. *101 Hymn Stories.* Grand Rapids, Mich.: Kregel Publications, 1982.

_____. *101 More Hymn Stories.* Grand Rapids, Mich.: Kregel Publications, 1985.

Reynolds, William J. *Companion to Baptist Hymnal.* Nashville, Tenn.: Broadman Press, 1976.

Sydnor, James. *Hymns and Their Uses.* Carol Stream, Ill.: Hope Publishing Co, 1982.

Music and Worship

Allen, Ronald, and Gordon Borror. *Worship: Rediscovering the Missing Jewel.* Portland, Oreg.: Multnomah Press, 1982.

Boschman, LaMar. *The Rebirth of Music.* Little Rock, Ark.: Manasseh Books, 1980.

Brant, Roxanne. *Ministering to the Lord.* Kirkwood, Mo.: Impact Books, 1973. Roxanne Brant Ministries, P.O. Box 1000, O'Brian, Fla. 32071.

Coleman, Michael, and Ed Lindquist. *Come and Worship: Tap into God's Power through Praise and Worship.* Old Tappan, N.J.: Fleming H. Revell Co., 1989.

Cornwall, Judson. *David Worshiped a Living God.* Shippensburg, Pa.: Destiny Image Publishers, 1989, (800) 722-6774.

_____. *Elements of Worship.* South Plainfield, N.J.: Bridge Publishing, Inc., 1985.

_____. *Let Us Draw Near.* South Plainfield, N.J.: Logos International, 1977.

_____. *Let Us Praise.* South Plainfield, N.J.: Logos International, 1973.

_____. *Worship as David Lived It.* Shippensburg, Pa.: Destiny Image Publishers, 1990.

Hayford, Jack W. *Worship His Majesty.* Waco, Tex.: Word, 1987.

Jackson, Mark. *Song Leader: Teaching the Church to Sing.* Schaumburg, Ill.: Regular Baptist, 1991.

Kendrick, Graham. *Learning to Worship as a Way of Life.* Minneapolis, Minn.: Bethany House Publishers, 1984.

Law, Terry. *The Power of Praise and Worship.* Tulsa, Okla.: Victory House Publishers, Inc., P.O. Box 700238, Tulsa, Okla. 74170, 1985.

_____. *Praise Releases Faith.* Tulsa, Okla.: Victory House Publishers, Inc., P.O. Box 700238, Tulsa, Okla. 74170, 1987.

Lovelace, Austin C., and William C. Rice. *Music and Worship in the Church.* Nashville, Tenn.: Abingdon Press, 1960.

Martin, Ralph. *The Worship of God.* Grand Rapids, Mich.: William B. Eerdmans Publishing Co., 1982.

Nori, Don. *His Manifest Presence.* Shippensburg, Pa.: Destiny Image Publishers, 1988.

Ortland, Anne. *Up with Worship: How to Quit Playing Church.* Ventura, Calif.: Regal Books, 1982.

Osbeck, Kenneth W. *The Endless Song: Music and Worship in the Church.* Grand Rapids, Mich.: Kregel Publications, 1987.

Schaeffer, Franky. *Addicted to Mediocrity: 20th-Century Christians and the Arts.* Westchester, Ill.: Crossway Books, 1981.

Sorge, Bob. *Exploring Worship: A Practical Guide to Praise and Worship.* Canandaigua, N.Y.: By the author, 236 Gorham St., Canandaigua, N.Y. 14424, 1987.

Taylor, Jack R. *The Hallelujah Factor: An Adventure into the Principles and Practice of Praise.* Nashville, Tenn.: Broadman Press, 1983.

Tozer, A. W. *Worship: The Missing Jewel of the Evangelical Church.* Camp Hill, Pa.: Christian Publications, 1979.

Wainwright, Geoffrey. *Doxology: The Praise of God in Worship, Doctrine, and Life.* New York: Oxford University Press, 1980.

Wardle, Terry Howard. *Exalt Him! Designing Dynamic Worship Services.* Camp Hill, Pa.: Christian Publications, 1988.

Webber, Robert E. *Worship Old and New.* Grand Rapids, Mich.: Zondervan Publishing House, 1982.

Weems, Ann. *Reaching for Rainbows.* Philadelphia, Pa.: The Westminster Press, 1980.

White, James F. *An Introduction to Christian Worship.* Nashville, Tenn.: Abingdon Press, 1980.

_____. *Protestant Worship: Traditions in Transition.* Louisville, Ky.: Westminster/John Knox Press, 1989.

Wyrtzen, Don. *A Musician Looks at the Psalms.* Grand Rapids, Mich.: Zondervan Publishing House, 1988.

Musicianship: Conducting, Vocal, and Instrumental Techniques

Apel, Willi. *Harvard Dictionary of Music.* Cambridge, Mass.: Harvard University Press, 1969.

Appelman, D. Ralph. *The Science of Vocal Pedagogy.* Bloomington, Ind.: Indiana University Press, 1967.

Boyd, Jack. *Rehearsal Guide for the Choir Director.* West Nyack, N.Y.: Parker Publishing Co., 1977.

Christy, Van A. *Expressive Singing.* Dubuque, Iowa: Wm. C. Brown Co., 1975.

_____. *Foundations in Singing.* Dubuque, Iowa: Wm. C. Brown Co., 1981.

Decker, Harold, and Julius Herford, eds. *Choral Conducting Symposium.* 2d ed. Englewood Cliffs:, N.J. Prentice-Hall, Inc., 1988.

Eskew, Harry. *Sing with Understanding.* Nashville, Tenn.: Broadman Press, 1980.

Fenton, William A., and Sarah O. Johnson. *Choral Musicianship: A Director's Guide to Better Singing.* Lebanon, Ind.: Houston Publishing, Inc., 1990.

Fischer, J. Cree. *Piano Turning: A Simple and Accurate Method for Amateurs.* New York: Dover Publications, Inc., 1976.

Green, Elizabeth A. H. *The Modern Conductor.* 2d ed. Englewood Cliffs, N.J.: Prentice-Hall, Inc., 1969.

Haasemann, Frauke, and James M. Jordan. *Group Vocal Techniques.* Chapel Hill, N.C.: Hinshaw Music, 1990.

_____. *Orchestral Bowings and Routines.* Ann Arbor, Mich.: Ann Arbor Publishers, 1990.

Henderson, Laura Browning. *How to Train Singers.* West Nyack, N.Y.: Parker Publishing Co., Inc., 1979.

Kennan, Kent. *The Technique of Orchestration.* Englewood Cliffs, N.J.: Prentice-Hall, 1990.

Marshall, Madeline. *The Singer's Manual of English Diction.* New York: Schirmer Books, 1953.

McKinney, James C. *The Diagnosis and Correction of Vocal Faults.* Nashville, Tenn.: Broadman Press, 1982.

Miller, Kenneth E. *Vocal Music Education.* Englewood Cliffs, N.J.: Prentice-Hall, Inc., 1988.

Mills, Elizabeth, and Sr. Therese Cecile Murphy, eds. *The Suzuki Concept: An Introduction to a Successful Method for Early Music Education.* Berkeley, Calif.: Diablo Press, 1973.

Osbeck, Kenneth W. *Pocket Guide for the Church Choir Member.* Grand Rapids, Mich.: Kregel Publications, 1984.

Piston, Walter. *Orchestration*. New York: W. W. Norton and Co., 1955.

Roe, Paul F. *Choral Music Education*. Englewood Cliffs, N.J.: Prentice-Hall, Inc., 1983.

Scherchen, Hermann. *Handbook of Conducting*. London: Oxford University Press, 1990.

Stanton, Royal. *The Dynamic Choral Conductor*. Delaware Water Gap, Pa.: Shawnee Press, 1971.

Uris, Dorothy. *To Sing in English*. New York: Boosey and Hawkes, 1971.

Vennard, William. *Singing, the Mechanism and the Technic*. New York: Fischer, Inc., 1967.

Organization and Time Management

Aslett, Don. *Clutter's Last Stand*. Cincinnati, Ohio: Writer's Digest Books, 1990.

Culp, Stephanie. *Conquering the Paper Pile-Up*. Cincinnati, Ohio: Writer's Digest Books, 1990.

_____. *How to Conquer Clutter*. Cincinnati, Ohio: Writer's Digest Books, 1989.

_____. *How to Get Organized When You Don't Have the Time*. Cincinnati, Ohio: Writer's Digest Books, 1986.

Fanning, Tony and Robbie. *Get It All Done and Still Be Human*. Cincinnati, Ohio: Writer's Digest Books, 1990.

Hemphill, Barbara. *Taming the Paper Tiger*. Cincinnati, Ohio: Writer's Digest Books, 1990.

Hendrick, Lucy. *Five Days to an Organized Life*. Cincinnati, Ohio: Writer's Digest Books, 1990.

Kotter, John P. *A Force for Change: How Leadership Differs from Management*. New York: Free Press, 1990.

Winston, Stephanie. *Getting Organized*. New York: Warner Books, 1978.

Other Books of Interest to Music Ministers

Eiche, Jon F. *What's a Synthesizer?* Milwaukee, Wis.: Hal Leonard Publishing Corp., 7777 West Bluemount Road, P.O. Box 13819, Milwaukee, Wis. 53213, 1987.

Freff, K. Kimball Holland, ed. *What's a Sampler?* Milwaukee, Wis.: Hal Leonard Publishing Corp., 7777 West Bluemount Road, P.O. Box 13819, Milwaukee, Wis. 53213, 1989.

Green, Melody, and David Hazard. *No Compromise: The Life Story of Keith Green*. Chatsworth, Calif.: Sparrow Press/The Sparrow Corp., 1989.

Hammar, Richard R., J.D., LL.M., CPA. *Church and Clergy Tax Guide.* Christian Ministry Resources, P.O. Box 2301, Matthews, N.C. 28106.

_____. *The Church Guide to Copyright Law.* Christian Ministry Resources, P.O. Box 2301, Matthews, N.C. 28106.

Hughes, Kent and Barbara. *Liberating Ministry from the Success Syndrome.* Wheaton, Ill.: Tyndale House, 1988.

Menconi, Al. *Today's Music: A Window to Your Child's Soul.* Elgin, Ill.: Lifejourney Books/David C. Cook Publishing Co., 1990.

Montgomery, Charles. *The Choir Director's Handbook?* [Humor] Nashville, Tenn.: Light Headed Music Publishing Co./A Division of Light Hearted Music Publishing Co., P.O. Box 150246, Nashville, Tenn. 37215, (615) 776-5678, 1984.

Pahlen, Kurt. *The World of the Oratorio.* Portland, Oreg.: Amadeus Press, 1990.

Riggs, R. M. *The Spirit-Filled Pastor's Guide.* Springfield, Mo.: Gospel Publishing House, 1948.

Robbins, Paul. *When It's Time to Move.* Carol Stream, Ill.: Leadership Library/Christianity Today, Inc., distributed by Word Books, 1985.

Roper, David. *A Burden Shared: Encouragement for Leaders.* Grand Rapids, Mich.: Discovery House Publishers, P.O. Box 3566, Grand Rapids, Mich. 49501, (800) 283-8333.

Sugden, Howard F., and Warren W. Wiersbe. *Confident Pastoral Leadership.* Chicago, Ill.: Moody Press, 1977.

Weeden, Larry, ed. *The Magnetic Fellowship.* Carol Stream, Ill.: Leadership Library/Christianity Today, Inc., distributed by Word Books, 1988.

Relationships

Berne, Eric. *Games People Play.* New York: Ballantine Books, 1964.

Berne, Eric, and Claude M. Steiner. *Beyond Games and Scripts.* New York: Ballantine Books, 1976.

Bramson, Robert M. *Coping with Difficult People.* New York: Ballantine Books, 1981.

Buckingham, Michele, ed. *Help! I'm a Pastor's Wife!* Altamonte Springs, Fla.: Strang Publishing Co., 1987.

Campbell, David. *If I'm in Charge Here, Why Is Everybody Laughing?* Niles, Ill.: Argus Communications, 1980.

Caruso, Beverly. *Loving Confrontation.* Minneapolis, Minn.: Bethany House Publishers, 1988.

Coble, Betty. *The Private Life of the Minister's Wife.* Nashville, Tenn.: Broadman, 1991.

Dale, Robert D. *Surviving Difficult Church Members.* Nashville, Tenn.: Abingdon Press, 1984.

Diehm, William J. *Criticizing.* Minneapolis, Minn.: Augsburg Publishing, 1986.

Exley, Richard. *Perils of Power.* Tulsa, Okla.: Harrison House, 1988.

_____. *The Rhythm of Life.* Tulsa, Okla.: Harrison House, 1987.

Fast, Julius. *Body Language.* New York: Pocket Books, 1970.

Faulkner, Brooks. *Burnout in Ministry.* Nashville, Tenn.: Broadman Press, 1991.

Haugk, Kenneth C. *Antagonists in the Church.* Minneapolis, Minn.: Augsburg, 1988.

Langberg, Diane. *Counsel for Pastors' Wives.* Grand Rapids, Mich.: Zondervan, 1988.

MacDonald, Gail. *High Call, High Privilege.* Wheaton, Ill.: Tyndale House Publishers, n.d.

Mayhall, Carole. *Words That Hurt, Words That Heal.* Colorado Springs, Colo.: Navpress, 1986.

Merrill, Dean. *Clergy Couples in Crisis.* Carol Stream, Ill.: Leadership Library/Christianity Today, Inc., distributed by Word Books, 1985.

Miller, Kevin A. *Secrets of Staying Power.* Carol Stream, Ill.: Leadership Library/Christianity Today, Inc., distributed by Word Books, 1988.

Montgomery, Shirley. *A Growth Guide for Ministers' Wives.* Nashville, Tenn.: Broadman Press, 1984.

_____. *Winning Ways for Ministers' Wives.* Nashville, Tenn.: Broadman Press, 1987.

Norheim, Karen. *Mrs. Preacher.* Joplin, Mo.: College Publishing Co., Inc., 1985.

Potter, Beverly. *Beating Job Burnout.* New York: Ace Books, 1980.

Senter, Ruth. *The Guilt-Free Book for Pastors' Wives.* Wheaton, Ill.: Victor Books, 1990.

Shelley, Marshall. *The Healthy, Hectic Home.* Carol Stream, Ill.: Leadership Library/Christianity Today, Inc., distributed by Word Books, 1988.

_____. *Helping Those Who Don't Want Help.* Carol Stream, Ill.: Leadership Library/Christianity Today, Inc., distributed by Word Books, 1986.

_____. *Well-Intentioned Dragons: Ministering to Problem People in the Church.* Carol Stream, Ill.: Leadership Library/Christianity Today, Inc., distributed by Word Books, 1985.

Smith, Fred. *Learning to Lead.* Carol Stream, Ill.: Leadership Library/Christianity Today, Inc., distributed by Word Books, 1986.

Strauss, Richard and Mary. *When Two Walk Together*. San Bernardino, Calif.: Here's Life Publishers, 1988.

Voges, Ken, and Ron Braund. *Understanding How Others Misunderstand You*. Chicago, Ill.: Moody Press, 1990.

White, Ruthe. *What Every Pastor's Wife Should Know*. Wheaton, Ill.: Tyndale House Publishers, 1986.

Sound, Lighting, and Drama

Allensworth, Carl, with Dorothy Allensworth and Clayton Rawson. *The Complete Play Production Handbook*. New York: Harper and Row Publ., 1982.

Bennett, Gordon C. *Readers Theatre Comes to Church*. Colorado Springs, Colo.: Meriwether Publishing Ltd., 1985.

Buerki, F. A. *Stagecraft for Non-Professionals*. Madison, Wis.: University of Wisconsin Press, Box 1379, Madison, Wis. 53701, 1972.

Craig-Claar, Deborah. *What to Do with the Second Shepherd on the Left*. Kansas City, Mo.: Lillenas Publication Co., 1992.

Eargle, John. *The Microphone Handbook*. Commack, N.Y.: Elar Publishing, 1982.

Everest, F. Alton. *The Master Handbook of Acoustics*. 2d ed. Blue Ridge Summit, Pa.: TAB Books, 1989.

Fuchs, Theodore. *Stage Lighting*. Boston, Mass.: Little, Brown, and Co., 1929.

Huber, David Miles. *Microphone Manual—Design and Application*. Indianapolis, Ind.: Howard W. Sams and Co., 1988.

McCandless, Stanley. *A Method of Lighting the Stage*. New York: Theater Arts Books, 1932.

Miller, James Hull. *Stagelighting in the Boondocks*. 2d ed. Contemporary Drama Service. Downers Grove, Ill.: Arthur Meriwether Publishers, 1981.

Novelly, Maria C. *Theatre Games for Young Performers*. Colorado Springs, Colo.: Meriwether Publishing Ltd., 1985.

Reid, Francis. *The Stage Lighting Handbook*. New York: Theater Arts Books, 1976.

Smith, Judy Gattis. *Drama through the Church Year*. Colorado Springs, Colo.: Meriwether Publishing Ltd., 1984.

Women in Leadership

Cannie, Joan Koob. *The Woman's Guide to Management Success*. Englewood Cliffs, N.J.: Prentice-Hall, Inc., 1979.

COMPUTER SOFTWARE

O "The Church Musician 2.0." Macintosh. "The Church Musician 3.0." IBM. Nine library files: "Octavo," "Collection," "Orchestration," "Bell Choir," "Record," "Trax," "Video," and "Equipment," "Personnel File"; "Custom Report Writer"; plus a directory of publishers, distributors, and dealers. Tempo Music Publications, Inc., 3773 W. 95th Street, Leawood, Kans. 66206, (913) 381-5088.

"ConcertWare + 4.0" and "ConcertWare + MIDI 5.0." Macintosh. Great Wave Software, 5353 Scotts Valley Drive, Scotts Valley, Calif. 95066, (408) 438-1990.

"Encore." Macintosh. Passport Designs, Inc., 100 Stone Pine Road, Half Moon Bay, Calif. 94019, (415) 726-0280.

O "Finale." Macintosh and IBM. Music writing with computer and MIDI keyboard. Tempo Music Publications, Inc., 3773 W. 95th Street, Leawood, Kans. 66206, (913) 381-5088.

O "HymnIndex." Macintosh and IBM. Index of hymns. HymnIndex Corporation, Box 9244, Greensboro, N.C. 27429, (919) 282-9220 or (800) 282-9220.

O "HymnSearch." Index of hymns. Tempo Music Publications, Inc., 3773 W. 95th Street, Leawood, Kans. 66206, (913) 381-5088.

"INFOsearch Hymnal for Worship and Celebration." IBM. Index for *Hymnal for Worship and Celebration* plus 11 other hymnals. NavPress Software, 1934 Rutland Drive, Suite 500, Austin, Tex. 78758, (800) 888-9898.

O "MusicBase Software." IBM. Available "libraries": "Music Library," "Hymnal Library," "Chorus Library," "Instrumental Library," "The Church Musician Magazine Library," "Periodical Library." "The Master Musician" contains all libraries. Southern Baptist Sunday School Board publications. SoftRay Resources, P.O. Box 5345, North Charleston, S.C. 29406, (803) 554-5130.

"Music Engraver 1.23." Macintosh. Music Environment, Inc., 4156 S. Mobile Cir., Aurora, Colo. 80013.

"Music Printer Plus." IBM. Tempo Music Publications, Inc., 3773 W. 95th Street, Leawood, Kans. 66206, (913) 381-5088.

"MusicProse." Macintosh. Coda Music Technology, 6210 Bury Drive, Eden Prairie, Minn. 55346, (800) 843-2066, fax: (612) 854-4631.

"The Music Secretary." IBM. Includes: "Master Member File," "Master Organization File," "Individual Organization File," "Music Library System," and "Congregation Music System." J and J Music, 234 Craft Hwy., Chickasaw, Ala. 36611, (800) 456-4966.

"MusicWriter Plus." IBM. Music notation. America's Music Service, 2000A Denison, Denton, Tex. 76201, (817) 898-1561 or (800) 235-5636.

"RapidPlanner." IBM. Worship planning program. RapidPlanner, 2110 Chase Crossing, Shreveport, La. 71118, (800) 673-3199.

"WinSong." IBM. WinSong, Inc., 5085 List Drive, Colorado Springs, Colo. 80919, (719) 593-9540.

CONFERENCES AND WORKSHOPS

Christian Artists' Music Seminar in the Rockies. Annual. Christian Artists Corporation, P.O. Box 338950, Denver, Colo. 80233, (800) 755-7464.

Church Music Explosion. Annual. Coral Ridge Presbyterian Church, 5555 N. Federal Hwy., Fort Lauderdale, Fla. 33308, (305) 771-8840.

Church Music in the Smokies. Annual. J and J Music, 234 Craft Hwy., Chickasaw, Ala. 36611, (800) 456-4966.

Hosanna. Annual. Alexandria House Choral Festival, 8225 Worthington-Galena Road, Westerville, Ohio 43081, (614) 431-8222.

MUSICalifornia. Annual. P.O. Box 8118, Mission Hills, Calif. 91346, (818) 993-8378.

Music, Drama, and Worship Conference. Annual. Kathy Suffridge, Lillenas Publishing, Box 419527, Kansas City, Mo. 64141, (800) 877-0700.

Music Florida. Annual. Kempke's Music Service, 2005 Tree Fork Lane, Suite 105, Longwood, Fla. 32750, (800) 753-6753.

Music Texas. Annual. Kempke's Music Service, 2005 Tree Fork Lane, Suite 105, Longwood, Fla. 32750, (800) 753-6753.

National Church Music Conference. Annual. Don Brandon, First Christian Church, 2600 Cleveland Avenue NW, Canton, Ohio 44709, (216) 456-2600.

DIRECTORIES, CATALOGS, AND MISCELLANEOUS RESOURCES

American Musical Supply Musician's Discount Catalog, 235 Franklin Avenue, Ridgewood, N.J. 07450-3295, (800) 458-4076.

Arthur Davenport and Associates. Choir enrollment and recruitment programs. P.O. Box 18545, Oklahoma City, Okla. 73154, (405) 528-4591 or (800) 654-8431.

Called Together Ministries' Guide to Support Resources for Clergy. Called Together Ministries, 20820 Avis Avenue, Torrance, Calif. 90503, (310) 793-9747.

Called Together Ministries Listening Line. A confidential telephone peer counseling service for clergy family members. (310) 793-9747. Hours: 10 A.M.–2 P.M. (Pacific time), Mon. through Sat.

The Christian Music Directories—Printed Music. Resource Publications, 160 E. Virginia Street #290, San Jose, Calif. 95112-58476, (800) 736-7600.

The Christian Music Directories—Recorded Music. Resource Publications, 160 E. Virginia Street #290, San Jose, Calif. 95112-5876, (800) 736-7600.

The Christian Music Industry Directory (1993 Edition). Sunshine Publishing Co., P.O. Box 45678, Baton Rouge, La. 70895, (504) 273-0161.

Friendship House Catalog. Musical gifts and awards. 29313 Clemens Road #2-G, P.O. Box 450978, Cleveland, Ohio 44145-0623, (216) 871-8040.

Gamble Music Co. Catalog. A/V equipment, band and choir equipment, instruments, risers, music education materials, awards, etc. Gamble Music Co., 312 South Wabash Avenue, Chicago, Ill. 60604, (800) 621-4290 or in Illinois: (800) 421-4484.

Gene Johnson Productions. Music stands, batons, music filing boxes and folders, etc. P.O. Box 3520, Estes Park, Colo. 80517, (800) 234-4363.

General Music Store Catalog. Instruments and supplies for education and entertainment. 19880 State Line Road, South Bend, Ind. 46637, (219) 272-8266 or (800) 348-5003.

Music in Motion Catalog. Music education and gifts. 783 North Grove, Suite 108, Richardson, Tex. 75081, (800) 445-0649 or in Texas: (214) 231-0403.

The Music Stand Catalog. Gifts from the performing arts. 1 Rockdale Plaza, Lebanon, N.H. 03766, (802) 295-7044.

Norcostco Catalog for the Performing Arts, 3203 North Highway 100, Minneapolis, Minn. 55422-9975, (612) 533-2791.

The Resource Guide. Gospel Music Association listing of artists, agents, festivals/events, music publishers, ministry organizations, etc. G.M.A., P.O. Box 23201, Nashville, Tenn. 37202-3201, (615) 242-0303.

Wenger Corporation Distinctive Equipment for Church Musicians Catalog, Dept. 44J, P.O. Box 448, Owatonna, Minn. 55060-0448, (800) 533-0393.

West Music Company Catalog. Rhythm and Orff instruments, recorders, keyboards, music education books and tapes. West Music Co., Box 5521, Coralville, Iowa 52241, (319) 351-0482 or (800) 397-9378.

FOR THE SMALL CHURCH

Music Rental and Resale

Choral Music Rental/Resale Library. Young's Music Store, Inc., 283 Fifth Street, Whitehall, Pa. 18052, (215) 437-3211 or (800) 628-6204.

The Music Library, 2509 Brittany Drive, Nashville, Tenn. 37206, (615) 226-5422.

The Sounding Board. Listing in: The Church Music Report, P.O. Box 1179, Grapevine, Tex. 76051-1179, (817) 488-0141.

Simple Choral Arrangements

Choral arrangements for 2-part choirs by The Music Sculptors. Sparrow Corporation, P.O. Box 2120, Chatsworth, Calif. 91311.

"You Can" series. Simple choral arrangements made available in a kit which includes ten books, one demo cassette, one accompaniment trax, three posters, clip art, sermon outline, suggestions, and instructions. Genevox Music, 127 Ninth Avenue N., Nashville, Tenn. 37234, (615) 251-2900 or (800) 251-3225.

MAGAZINES AND NEWSLETTERS

Church Music

The Church Musician. Southern Baptist music leaders. 127 Ninth Avenue N., Nashville, Tenn. 37234, (615) 251-2961 or (800) 458-2772.

The Church Music Report, P.O. Box 1179, Grapevine, Tex. 76099-1179, (817) 488-0141, fax: (817) 481-4191.

Church Music Workshop. United Methodist Publishing House. Magazine, music folio, and audiocassette. Cokesbury Subscription Services, P.O. Box 801, Nashville, Tenn. 37202-0801, (800) 672-1789.

The Communicator. J and J Music, P.O. Box 11468, Chickasaw, Ala. 36611, (205) 452-2000 or (800) 456-4966.

Creator. The bimonthly magazine of balanced music ministries. P.O. Box 100, Dublin, Ohio 43017, (614) 777-7774.

The Hymn. Hymn Society of America. Southwestern Baptist Theological Seminary, P.O. Box 22000, Fort Worth, Tex. 76122, (800) 843-4966.

The Music Leader. Southern Baptist Convention. 127 Ninth Avenue N., Nashville, Tenn. 37234, (800) 458-2772.

Music Makers. Southern Baptist Convention. 127 Ninth Avenue N., Nashville, Tenn. 37234, (800) 458-2772.

Music Revelation, 7 Elmwood Court, Rockville, Md. 20850, (301) 424-2956.

Music Time. Southern Baptist Convention. 127 Ninth Avenue N., Nashville, Tenn. 37234, (800) 458-2772.

Note This. Bimonthly newsletter of the National Music Department of the Assemblies of God. 1445 Boonville Avenue, Springfield, Mo. 65802-1894, (417) 862-2781.

Quarter Notes. For leaders of music with children. United Methodist Publishing House, Graded Press, 201 Eighth Avenue S., P.O. Box 801, Nashville, Tenn. 37202, (800) 672-1789.

Radiant Music Leadership Training Series. Assemblies of God National Music Department, 1445 Boonville Avenue, Springfield, Mo. 65802, (417) 862-2781.

Sing! Jr. A newsletter for children's choirs and their families. P.O. Box 5191, Belmont, Calif. 94002, (415) 349-9784.

Sing! The Choir's Resource. An international monthly newsletter for church choirs. P.O. Box 5191, Belmont, Calif. 94002, (415) 349-9784.

Take Note. A quarterly newsletter for music staff from Christian Supply. Christian Supply, Inc., P.O. Box 4009, Spartanburg, S.C. 29305, (800) 952-6657.

Young Musicians. Southern Baptist Convention. 127 Ninth Avenue N., Nashville, Tenn. 37203, (800) 458-2772.

Ministry

Advance. For ministers and church leaders. Assemblies of God, 1445 Boonville Avenue, Springfield, Mo. 65802, (417) 862-2781.

Baptist Leader, P.O. Box 851, Valley Forge, Pa. 19482-0851, (215) 768-2153.

The Christian Ministry. The Christian Century Foundation, 407 S. Dearborn Street, Suite 1405, Chicago, Ill. 60605, (312) 427-5380.

Church Administration. For Southern Baptist pastors, staff, and volunteer church leaders. 127 Ninth Avenue N., Nashville, Tenn. 37234, (615) 251-2062 or (800) 458-2772.

Church Educator. Creative resources for christian educators. Educational Ministries, Inc., 165 Plaza Drive, Prescott, Ariz. 86303, (800) 221-0910.

The Clergy Journal. Church Management, Inc., P.O. Box 6160, Carmen Ave. East, Inver Grove Heights, Minn. 55076-9909, (800) 328-0200.

Discipleship Training. For workers and leaders in the church training program of the Southern Baptist Convention. 127 Ninth Avenue N., Nashville, Tenn. 37234, (615) 251-2843 or (800) 458-2772.

Evangelizing Today's Child. Child Evangelism Fellowship, Inc., Warrenton, Mo. 63383-3420, (314) 456-4321.

Group Magazine. Youth ministry. 2890 N. Monroe, Box 481, Loveland, Colo. 80539, (303) 669-3836 or (800) 447-1070.

Group's Junior High Ministry Magazine. Group Publishing, 2890 N. Monroe, Box 481, Loveland, Colo. 80539, (303) 669-3836 or (800) 447-1070.

Growing Churches. For Southern Baptist pastors, staff, and volunteer church leaders. 127 Ninth Avenue N., Nashville, Tenn. 37234, (615) 251-2062 or (800) 458-2772.

Leader. Board of Christian Education of the Church of God, P.O. Box 2458, Anderson, Ind. 46018-2458, (317) 642-0255.

Leadership. A practical journal for church leaders. Subscription Service, P.O. Box 11618, Des Moines, Iowa 50340, (800) 777-3136.

Lutheran Forum. For Lutheran church leadership, clerical and lay. The Wartburg, Bradley Avenue, Mt. Vernon, N.Y. 10552.

Ministries Today. The magazine about renewal in leadership. Ministries Today, P.O. Box 549, Mt. Morris, Ill. 61054, (800) 877-5334.

The Preacher's Magazine. Nazarene Publishing House, P.O. Box 419527, Kansas City, Mo. 64141, (800) 877-0700.

Serving Together. Called Together Ministries newsletter—resources and referrals for pastors' wives. 20820 Avis Avenue, Torrance, Calif. 90503, (310) 793-9747.

Sunday School Counselor. Assemblies of God, 1445 Boonville Avenue, Springfield, Mo. 65802, (417) 862-2781.

Teachers Interaction. A magazine church school workers grow by. Concordia Publishing House, 3558 S. Jefferson, St. Louis, Mo. 63118, (800) 325-3040.

Music

The American Organist. American Guild of Organists, 475 Riverside Drive, Suite 1260, New York, N.Y. 10115, (212) 870-2310.

American Songwriter, 27 Music Square E., Nashville, Tenn. 37203, (615) 244-6065.

The Choral Journal. American Choral Directors Association, P.O. Box 6310, Lawton, Okla. 73506.

Clavier. A magazine for pianists and organists. The Instrumental Co., 200 Northfield Road, Northfield, Ill. 60093, (708) 446-5000.

The Diapason, 380 Northwest Highway, Des Plaines, Ill. 60016-2282.

Guitar Player Magazine, 600 Harrison Street, San Francisco, Calif. 94107, (415) 905-2200.

The Instrumentalist. Instrumentalist Publishing Co., 200 Northfield Road, Northfield, Ill. 60093, (708) 446-5000.

International Musician. American Federation of Musicians, Paramount Building, Suite 600, 1501 Broadway, New York, N.Y. 10036, (212) 869-1330 or (800) 762-3444.

Modern Drummer, 870 Pompton Avenue, Cedar Grove, N.J. 07009, (201) 239-4140.

The Monitor. Peavey Electronics Corporation, 711 A Street, Meridian, Miss. 39301, (601) 483-5365.

Musical America, 825 Seventh Avenue, New York, N.Y. 10019.

Music Educators Journal. Music Educators National Conference, 1201 16th Street NW, Washington, Tenn. 37203.

Musician. Billboard Publications, 1515 Broadway, 39th Floor, New York, N.Y. 10036, (212) 536-5208.

Sounding Board. K and R Music Inc., P.O. Box 616, Trumansburg, N.Y. 14886, (607) 387-5775.

The Vocal Coach. Chris and Carole Beatty. StarSong, 2325 Crestmoor, Nashville, Tenn. 37215, (615) 269-0196.

Worship

The Psalmist. Psalmist Reources/Kent Henry Ministries, 9820 East Watson, St. Louis, Mo. 63126, (314) 842-6161 or (800) 343-9933.

Worship Times. The International Worship Resource Network, P.O. Box 31050, Laguna Hills, Calif. 92654, (800) 245-7664.